Citicorp

Other Books by Richard B. Miller

American Banking in Crisis

The Bankers Desk Book

The Banking Yearbook

Super Banking

Tax Haven Investing

The Banking Jungle (coauthored with Paul Nadler)

Ghost Towns of California

Citicorp

The Story of
a Bank in Crisis

Richard B. Miller

McGraw-Hill, Inc.

New York   San Francisco   Washington, D.C.   Auckland   Bogotá
Caracas   Lisbon   London   Madrid   Mexico City   Milan
Montreal   New Delhi   San Juan   Singapore
Sydney   Tokyo   Toronto

Library of Congress Cataloging-in-Publication Data

Miller, Richard Bradford.
    Citicorp : the story of a bank in crisis / Richard B. Miller.
        p.   cm.
    Includes index.
    ISBN 0-07-042340-7 :
    1. Citicorp—History. I. Title.
HG2613.N54C7236   1993
332.1´22´0973—dc20   92-32533
                                                 CIP

1 2 3 4 5 6 7 8 9 0 DOC/DOC 9 9 8 7 6 5 4 3

ISBN   0-07-042340-7

The sponsoring editor for this book was Theodore C. Nardin, the editing supervisor was Jane Palmieri, and the production supervisor was Pamela Pelton. It was set in Palatino by McGraw-Hill's Professional Book Group composition unit.

Printed and bound by R. R. Donnelley & Sons Company.

This book is printed on recycled, acid-free paper containing a minimum of 50% recycled de-inked fiber.

Contents

Preface

Citicorp, combined with its lead bank, Citibank, and its hundreds of subsidiaries here and abroad, is a world-class financial institution. It is also a corporation with world-class problems.

Any business organization, of course, has problems, some of them big and some of them small. This has certainly been the case at Citicorp right from its beginnings back in 1812. During the period of its most spectacular growth, under the leadership of Walter Wriston, there were all sorts of problems, although none of them life-threatening. And when that era ended in the mid-1980s, Citi was in generally good shape, with its overall performance moving forward in a positive direction, toward new highs.

By and large, that forward performance continued under the new leadership of John Reed for a few more years, until near the end of the 1980s. Then cracks appeared in the seemingly invincible world of Citicorp.

As a long-time observer of the banking industry—I began writing about banks more than a quarter of a century ago—Citicorp has always been a major player in the banking scene I have covered. Sometimes the news about Citicorp was exasperating (as when it made a move that might be described as too aggressive or even stupid); sometimes it was exhilarating (when it took a leading position in the industry or announced a spectacular new service). But no matter what occurred, Citicorp could never be described as being dull.

When Walter Wriston retired, all of banking wondered how a relatively young John Reed would do. Although he had been a leading player at Citi and in the industry for some time, he was still a fairly unknown quantity.

Yet when he took over the chairmanship of Citicorp, overnight he became the most powerful banker in the country, if not the world. Would he be able to fill the very large shoes of his predecessor, both literally and figuratively? His style could hardly have been more different from Wriston's, and he actively took steps to avoid the spotlight. But when Reed announced in 1987 that Citicorp was facing financial reality and would write off a substantial portion of its Latin American loans, he dramatically demonstrated to a great many people both inside and out of the banking industry that he had what it takes to run America's biggest banking company—or so most thought at the time.

However, other difficulties at Citicorp began to appear. There were the gnawing problems of inadequate capital resources, the subsidiaries that weren't making money, the increasing number of nonperforming loans, the burgeoning amount of foreclosed real estate properties, the hesitant managerial leadership, and the resulting reversal of the organization's financial performance.

Rumors of Reed's premature departure, and even of the bank's impending demise, began swirling around the industry and throughout the business world.

When BankAmerica was on the ropes during the mid-1980s, it appeared that Citicorp did not have to worry anymore about its most serious rival for U.S. banking supremacy. Citi, however, did not seize the opportunity that had presented itself, perhaps because of the need to focus on problems arising from its changing leadership. Later, as the crisis at Citi deepened, the bank was unable to take advantage of the void left by BankAmerica. Then, almost miraculously, BankAmerica recovered and again became a serious competitor. Not only that, several superregional banking organizations (Banc One, NationsBank) showed they could successfully cope with a poor economy and also began to move up and closer to a hurting Citicorp. Even two troubled banks right in Citi's own backyard (Chemical and Manufacturers Hanover) joined forces and found strength in unity, presenting Citi with yet another strong competitor.

With all this happening, it seemed an appropriate time to take a long, hard look at Citicorp—its past, its present, and its uncertain future. That is what this book does.

My first move was to talk with Citicorp management, and with John Reed in particular. Requests for interviews were rebuffed several times; in fact, no member of Citi's top management team would meet with me. And Walter Wriston, who still has an office in Citicorp Center, passed along word that he would follow Reed's lead. Of course, it is highly unlikely he would have criticized the performance of his hand-picked successor, even had he granted me a meeting.

So I talked with a great many other people—employees, former employees, other bankers, stock analysts, consultants, customers, etc. Information was gathered from countless other sources, and I wrote what turned out to be *Citicorp: The Story of a Bank in Crisis.* I have done whatever I reasonably could to make sure the information included herein is accurate and current, at least current as of the time this book went to the printers. If Mr. Reed and his associates have a different viewpoint, that certainly is their prerogative. If they possess information that would have altered what has been written, I am sorry they did not share it with me; I did what I could to gain their cooperation.

It is always unsettling to see an organization, in this case a great banking organization, beset with problems. Those who suffer the most in such instances are the stockholders and the employees. At Citi, the shareholders have seen the value of their investment decline, and thousands of employees have lost their jobs. Fortunately for Citicorp's customers and for the public in general, other banking institutions are taking up the slack. And a number of them doing quite well in the process; according to the latest statistics from the Federal Deposit Insurance Corporation, the insured commercial banks in the United States earned a record $7.2 billion in the second quarter of 1992. Citicorp has also moved back into the black this year, so it too is showing some signs of recovery, weak though those signs may be.

At the same time, there have been several unsettling stories about Citicorp during the late summer and early autumn of 1992—the restatement of its second-quarter earnings, the lower-than-expected third-quarter earnings, the need to check with the regulators before making acquisitions, the abrupt resignation of president Richard Braddock.

During these last few years, the banking industry has had more than its share of troubles. A great many banks have already failed, and undoubtedly more will fail in the months ahead. But still other banks have put their troubles behind them. As this book goes to press, it is clear that the crisis at Citicorp remains.

RICHARD B. MILLER
Cresskill, New Jersey
January 1993

Introduction: The World According to Citicorp

> I am perfectly confident that it is open to us to become the most powerful, the most serviceable, the most far-reaching financial institution that has ever been.

Those are not the words of Walter Wriston, who guided Citicorp to its position as the number-one bank here and in many parts of the world; nor were they uttered by the current (and currently beleaguered) Citicorp chairman John Reed before Citicorp's world began to crack. Those words were written back in 1915 by Frank Vanderlip who was then the president of the City Bank of New York in a letter to the chairman of the bank, James Stillman.

Over the years, the name of the bank evolved through mergers and acquisitions and just plain expansion to become Citibank and its holding company, Citicorp. But the thoughts Vanderlip expressed nearly 80 years ago have, to a considerable extent, molded the philosophy and governed the direction of the organization over the years and up into this last decade of the twentieth century. As a consequence of the bank's holding to this mission, there has never been a banking company in the United States with the size, the power, and the willingness to use its considerable resources for whatever purpose that even comes close to the organization known here and throughout the world as Citicorp.

In light of the harsh reality of the financial marketplace, together with the massive changes taking place internationally, chances are that there never will be a banking company of such magnitude again.

Based on recent events, sad to say, that sobering assessment would appear to include Citicorp itself, circa 1993.

Although it has achieved a great deal since its beginnings in 1812, this unique banking company has rarely, if ever, been called the best. That certainly is the case today. In fact, the respected investment firm of Keefe Bruyette & Woods ranks Citicorp first among the 50 largest banks in the United States in only one category—size. Performance is quite another matter. Keefe Bruyette ranks it forty-third in profits (the rankings were made prior to the 1991 financial reports; today that ranking would be still lower), and at the very bottom in risk-adjusted capital.

In its August 20, 1991, issue, *Financial World* magazine, using a complicated formula, places Citicorp 173d among the 219 largest U.S. banking institutions, thanks to such factors as a high percentage of nonperforming assets to total assets, and a low percentage of reserves to nonperforming assets. Other data reported by the magazine are equally devastating: a negative return on assets of −0.02 percent; also placing the market-economic value of its stock at 1906 percent (where 100 percent means the stock is fully valued). This latter figure means the market value is far above the economic value of the stock. Incidentally, the assets and stock price at the time the rankings were made were at approximately the same level as they were in the fall of 1992.

The world according to Citicorp has been a big and exciting world, but it has been far from perfect. Now that world is being altered, and this is happening in ways not all that pleasing to Citicorp management and staff members, who are shrinking in numbers, and stockholders, who presently are earning no dividends.

Pride and Performance

It must be said that during much of its 180-year history, Citicorp has performed far better than more recent results indicate. It has also survived, something an unfortunate number of banks have failed to do. This overall performance by Citicorp has been due, in no small part, to its good fortune in having strong, able leadership, both at the top and throughout its managerial ranks.

During the 1970s and into the 1980s, under the aggressive, savvy, and (sometimes) acerbic leadership of chairman and chief executive officer Walter Wriston, Citicorp grew rapidly, spreading its influence around the world, building on a strong base left him by his predecessor, George Moore. It was also during this period that the organization honed its reputation for ruthlessness and what some have described as a rather cavalier attitude toward restrictive regulation. Certainly there was an exasperation expressed by bank officials from time to time over the rules laid down by governments both here and abroad. The banking company, and its management, was bound and determined to be number one. Actually, during most of that period, it was not even the largest bank in the United States; Bank of America, based in San Francisco, was. Citicorp did not finally overtake Bank of America in terms of total assets until 1982, and it wasn't until 1985 that it moved ahead of its West Coast rival in total deposits.

While the amount of assets is probably a reasonably good indication of a bank's stature (certainly it provides a more precise statement of an organization's size and inherent power than do deposits), the figures provide but one measure of the bank's real position within the banking industry and the entire business community. It is what a bank actually does with those assets that demonstrates the real stature of the organization and determines the true role it will play within the industry and throughout the business world.

Without question, Citicorp management has been more than willing to use the strength of the organization to advance the cause of the company. Its leaders, most especially Wriston and Reed, have followed the musings of Frank Vanderlip, and they have seen their institution become "far-reaching" in every sense of the word.

A Record of Accomplishment

Citicorp has moved forcefully and purposefully throughout the world, doing business in an increasing number of countries far beyond what other U.S. banking institutions were (or are) doing—or probably even thought of doing.

At present, the organization has a network of about 3300 branches, offices, subsidiaries, and affiliates, spanning six continents and located in 92 countries. It has millions of customers in the United States alone, with offices in 34 states and the District of Columbia. Thanks to its credit card business (about 31 million people hold Citibank cards worldwide), which places it far ahead of any other bank, Citicorp wields enormous influence in the lives of the American public.

A 1991 survey by Goldman, Sachs and Company of chief financial officers at large U.S. firms showed that Citibank, the principal bank of the Citicorp holding company, has primary relationships with 41 percent of the participating companies. This is an increase from 27 percent in the previous year, a figure which places the bank far ahead of its nearest competitors.

Moreover, according to Citicorp-supplied statistics, Citibank has a banking relationship with one in four households in the United States, and it serves 39 percent of the households in the New York City market. It also is the leading servicer of home mortgages in the country; however, that is a fact that has not been all that advantageous to the bank during the last year or so.

Internationally, also according to Citicorp statistics, the organization's Citibank Private Bank is the largest non-Swiss bank of its kind in the world. (This unit has also been one of the more reliable sources of profit for the company in recent years.) In Japan, it is the leading and most profitable foreign bank; in fact, Citibank has become the only U.S. bank in that country with a substantial presence. And in Mexico, Citibank is the only privately owned international bank allowed to operate there.

In recent years, Citicorp has become the largest foreign-exchange trader in the world. Sometimes its efforts in this highly profitable area have been alleged to be overzealous (a situation which is described in Chapter 9), but they do seem to have paid off. The company's correspondent banking business, which for many years was never particularly remarkable, has recently grown substantially and is now far ahead of its competition.

Whereas Bank of America once was the leading consumer banking institution in the country, Citicorp adroitly took advantage of Bank of America's problems in the early 1980s and moved smartly ahead. Citicorp remains in first place today, although this position is being challenged by increasingly vigorous competitors (including the rejuvenated Bank of America); it is also being undermined by Citicorp's own, internal problems.

Closer to its home base, Citicorp and Chase Manhattan used to be bitter and fairly evenly matched competitors, each striving to be number one in New York City and throughout the world—but not in the rest of the United States, where Bank of America reigned supreme after World War II. In fact, back in the 1960s, both Citicorp and Chase were evenly matched in vying to end the year in first place in terms of assets and amount of deposits. In addition, both banking companies wanted to be known as international banks of the first rank; this was particularly so at Chase under David Rockefeller's leadership. Today, Chase has fallen far behind, both in New York and worldwide. Citicorp presently dominates the New York metropolitan market, although even in its hometown it is being briskly challenged. Its most prominent competitor today is Chemical Bank, which recently merged with Manufacturers Hanover Trust Company to form the second-largest bank in the city.

Citicorp has also been one of the most innovative corporations, banking or otherwise, in history. During the 1960s, it developed and popularized the certificate of deposit (CD); and in the 1970s, it was the first bank to aggressively market credit cards throughout the nation. Citicorp also was one of the first banking companies to see the advantages and the terrific potential of electronic funds transfers and other technological developments. As a result, the company left most other banks behind as it moved strongly and confidently into the age of electronics. And one of the Citicorp people leading the charge in this direction was its current chairman and chief executive officer, John Reed, who replaced Walter Wriston when the former chairman retired in mid-1984.

Even Citicorp Center, the headquarters office building in midtown Manhattan, which was dedicated in 1977, almost instantaneously became the recognizable symbol of the bank. For example, if there were no wording on the cover jacket of this book, you would know that it was about Citicorp. When first built, the building and its unique slanted top seemed to indicate that the organization was on the move and reaching for the sky. Of course, there are those who now say that the structure is an apt symbol of a company that is losing shape and sliding downhill.

All this just goes to show how things change.

The Harsh Realities

When John Reed succeeded Walter Wriston as CEO eight years ago, the future for Citicorp could not have been brighter. In fact, after just two years under Reed, the bank's 1986 income reached a record $1.028 billion. Although the new chief executive was far different from his predecessor in so many ways, including such attributes as managerial style and personality, it seemed at first that the baton had been passed without missing a beat.

The following year, 1987, the bank generally continued to perform well. At the same time, its annual report showed a whopping loss of $1.182 billion. This loss was due to a calculated decision to face up to the deterioration of its loan portfolio to less-developed countries (LDCs), a situation that promised to get far worse before it got better if it ever would. Reserves were augmented by $3.0 billion that year, which reduced earnings and equity by an equal amount. The result was the first loss for the bank since the depression year of 1934. (Citi weathered the Great Depression better than many banks of that period, though not without serious and long-lasting difficulties.) The stock dividend in 1987, however, was actually increased by 10 percent. And John Reed deservedly received high praise for biting the bullet on heavy concentration of LDC loans. Moreover (and to their credit), a great many other banks followed his lead. Citicorp stockholders, who might otherwise have been upset at the substantial loss posted, were undoubtedly mollified by the dividend increase. And, not incidentally, they appreciated the gutsy move on the LDC loans. By its actions, the board demonstrated its faith in John Reed and the future of the bank.

As it worked out, the following year was perhaps the highwater mark for the bank under its present leadership. Earnings in 1988 set a new record of $1.858 billion. Return on common stockholders' equity (ROE) was a spectacular 23.6 percent, a rate that few banks, large or small, ever come close to meeting.

But after 1988 things began to change—and far too many of those things not for the better. Since that year, Citicorp has been on a roller coaster ride heading downhill. That includes the price of its stock, which dropped to a low of $8.50 a share on December 20, 1991. It was in the $50 range when Reed took over. The stock rebounded into the low twenties during the middle of 1992 when earnings once again were in the black, but then it dropped below $15 during October following a series of negative developments. Even if the stock returns to the $20 range, it won't be close to what the price was during the summer of '84.

On the international financial scene, Citicorp has been having trouble keeping pace with the rest of the financial world. *American Banker*, the daily newspaper for the banking industry, puts Citicorp in twenty-first place among the largest banking institutions throughout the world. This is the first time that a U.S. bank has not ranked among the 20 largest. Why did this happen? There are any number of reasons, including such factors as inflation and the fact that many foreign banks enjoy government backing (for example, many foreign banks can own other kinds of businesses in their own countries)—factors over which Citicorp had or has little control. But it has also lost its ranking because of other factors, such as its inability to finance mergers and acquisitions with other banking institutions and to generate internal growth.

In many respects, Citicorp simply has not been moving forward. The total assets of just under $217 billion reported in 1991 is almost exactly the same as in 1990. The drop has been rather precipitous—in 1985, Citicorp was ranked number one in the world in asset size. Today, depending on what list you look at, Citi isn't even in the top 25. Oh, how the mighty have fallen—and in just eight years under John Reed.

The Wrong Kind of Turnaround

There is other evidence that Citicorp is actually moving in the opposite direction, becoming a smaller (and less powerful) bank. There were 95,000 employees worldwide at year-end 1990; at year-end 1991, that number had dropped to 86,000; at the end of 1992, that number was considerably lower. Much of this reduction has been, of course, part of a calculated move on the part of top management to cut expenses. There were also 2000 fewer stockholders in 1991 than in 1990. And Citicorp operated in 41 states during 1990; today, as previously noted, it is located in 7 fewer states.

In the area of personnel, more and sizeable staff reductions have been planned. But other people, important management people, have also been leaving, often on their own initiative, because of dissatisfaction with the Citicorp organization or for greater opportunities elsewhere. Some of this brain drain, of course, can be expected when a new regime takes over; for example, two of the three top contenders to replace Wriston (there were actually many more who were or could have been in the running, thanks to the company's managerial depth) have left Citicorp, as have several others in the layer of management just below the top level. But there have been other losses, often unplanned and unwanted, that indicate some deep divisions within the organization. The most recent example of this occurred in late September 1992, when Citicorp president Richard Braddock, who was a close associate of Reed and had been named to the position only two years before, unexpectedly resigned. The bank issued a statement that Braddock wanted "to pursue new career opportunities."

Until recently, the organization had worked to increase its size by acquiring other banks; by either buying or establishing bank-related businesses; and, of course, by making more loans and bringing in more deposits. The result had been a growth rate that was both spectacular and steady. The merger and purchase route has been abandoned of late, a move forced upon the organization because of a lack of profits and insufficient capital—and the almost foregone realization that regulatory approval of any expansion move would most likely be denied. This abandonment has occurred, unfortunately for Citicorp, at the very time that the banking industry has entered a new era of consolidation, with megamergers creating ever-larger banks and more tough competition for Citicorp.

Moreover, loans, both commercial and consumer, have been on the decrease, although this situation has undoubtedly been due as much to the state of the economy as to anything else. The organization's real estate loan portfolio, in particular, is in terrible shape, and has been for some time. Even those stock analysts who are cautiously optimistic about Citicorp since its earnings upswing in 1992 indicate that its real estate loans could be the bank's Achilles' heel. An improving economy will certainly improve some aspects of the bank's lending picture. However, the sorry state of Citicorp's total loan portfolio (which is readily discernable from the bank's financial statements) is but further evidence of a banking organization with major problems which must be solved—and solved fairly quickly—if it is to survive, much less maintain its place in the banking community.

A Different World

What has happened to this powerhouse of a bank? Where did it go wrong? Is senior management to blame? Is any one person to blame? What *is* the organization doing (if anything) to turn things around? Is what it *is* doing enough? Should action have been taken earlier? What will be the differences between the Citicorp of the 1970s and 1980s and the Citicorp of the 1990s? Or, for that matter, what will the bank be like after the turn of the twenty-first century? Will it be a kinder, gentler banking company tomorrow than it was yesterday?

Some of the problems facing Citicorp can be blamed on the recent recession, as has already been noted. But most of the difficulties—or, at least, the seriousness of those difficulties—are the responsibility of its management, past and present. Management must—and, indeed, should—accept the lion's share of the blame for the woes presently plaguing Citicorp.

John Reed has come under increasing criticism for the quality of his stewardship of the bank during the past eight years. But not all of the blame can be placed at Reed's feet. It wasn't he who was responsible for all those LDC loans; Walter Wriston was. Still, a strong case can be made that Reed did not act soon enough to address the other serious problems at Citicorp. And he most certainly waited too long before moving in his own management team. There is also growing concern that more drastic action is needed, beyond that which already has been done, or which is presently in the works, or which may even be contemplated.

Just how bad off is Citicorp? Is the bank, as some have intimated, insolvent? Is it now, or has it ever been, on the Federal Deposit Insurance Corporation's list of troubled banks? Is it possible that powerful Citicorp could fail—or, for that matter, would the government allow it to fail? Will it survive? And if it does, will it still bear some resemblance to the Citicorp of old?

These and other matters will be explored in this book about a great banking institution in deep trouble. The book begins with what surely is its most pressing problem—inadequate capital. Then the dreary state of Citi's loan portfolio will be explored. The final section in Part 1 will look at the organization's management. Part 2 will take a look at how a little New York City bank grew up to become Citicorp. And Part 3 will examine the elements that have contributed to the Citi image. Finally, the present situation and how it is impacting on Citicorp will complete the analysis and show how this banking organization no longer is what it used to be.

Certainly it is fair to say that Citicorp is not the same institution today as it was even five short years ago, and it will not be the same in five years as it is today. The company has been constantly evolving, and this will continue to be the case.

In many ways, Citicorp has had a hell of a ride; it was exhilarating, sometimes bumpy, sometimes close to the edge, yet almost always interesting. But that ride is over. Now it is striving to change course and get back on track for another, far different—and perhaps shorter—ride.

PART 1

Citicorp at the Brink

We have some chips in every game in town.
WALTER WRISTON
Euromoney, July 1978

The 1990s have not been kind to Citicorp. In fact, they have been downright brutal.

Of course, many of the problems that have come to light and/or to a head during the past couple of years actually had their origins during the 1980s and some even earlier than that. Unfortunately, several of those problems were not apparent then, or they have since grown and multiplied over the years. Today, as the bank and its stockholders have discovered, there simply is no way to escape these problems—they must be faced and they must be dealt with. The problems have decimated profits, restricted corporate moves, constricted the business, diminished the stature of the organization, and lowered expectations for the future.

The stage for all this was actually set as the 1980s came to a close. Although 1989 earnings were not much more than a quarter of the record high posted in 1988, Citicorp management did not appear to be particularly concerned with the drop. After all, deposits had increased substantially over the previous year and assets had reached an historic high of $230.6 billion. Part of the reason for the lower earnings, bank officials pointed out, was the investment in Quotron (a subsidiary that supplies stock quotes and other financial information),* plus something described in Citicorp's 1989 annual report as "an exciting new 'Point of Sale' initiative." That "point of sale" initiative, it is worth noting, apparently is a package of information services to assist businesses in consumer marketing, plus a business travel information service. Nearly three years later, the initiative is still in the development stage.†

Taking note of the risk-based capital guidelines that had been issued by the Federal Reserve and the other federal banking regulators, Citicorp officials observed that their institution met the then-current capital requirements and would have no trouble meeting the new minimum requirements for 1990 and, for that matter, the years beyond.

As if to demonstrate the inherent strength of the bank, the annual stock dividend was boosted by 14 cents per share, to $1.68. Indeed, this step apparently worked and the price of Citicorp stock increased in 1989, closing the year at $28.875 per share.

From time to time, there had been a few rumblings about the direction in which Citi seemed to be going and about John Reed's stewardship of the company. But it wasn't until 1990 that things began to unravel to the point where at least some concern began to be publicly expressed about various aspects of the bank's core businesses and several of its subsidiaries. Earnings remained essentially flat that year and deposits were somewhat higher, but assets dropped by $14 billion. Attempting to put a confident spin on what could only be described as a lackluster performance, Reed said in that year's annual report, "We end the year continuing to believe that Citicorp is one of the world's great banking institutions with a unique, and uniquely valuable franchise...."

Are these Frank Vanderlip's words updated to the 1990s?

At Long Last Action

Beginning in the fourth quarter of 1990, management started to take some steps they believed would help correct the increasingly evident deficiencies in performance and solve the mounting problems confronting the institution. It is not clear, however, how serious top management actually

*More about Quotron in Chapters 1 and 11.
†More about this initiative in Chapter 11.

considered the situation to be at that time. Much of what was done, or at least was planned, by the end of the year was tentative, and it was not particularly effective.

However, in 1991, Reed and his associates (finally) accepted the now-apparent fact that Citicorp was in considerable trouble and that there had to be some changes made.

Right after the beginning of the year, Citicorp installed what the corporation is calling its "five-point plan" to restore the bank's previous earnings momentum, improve its competitive stance, and increase capital strength. The plan was formulated to accomplish those goals within a two-year period, or by the end of 1992. The five points of the plan are

- Focus on 1991 and 1992
- Manage differently—to reduce the cost base and improve the relationship between revenue and expense
- Strengthen capital
- Build on its core businesses
- Maintain a strong customer focus

It seems obvious that this plan is rather diffuse, designed as much for its public relations value as for its attention to the real problems facing the organization. At the same time, even a flawed or inadequate plan is better than no plan at all. Now, close to two years later, that plan is still in place. Progress has been made on achieving the goals in each of the five points. Capital has been strengthened (see the next chapter), and costs have been reduced. The focus has been on the present, and there seems to be greater attention being paid to the customer. But is the company managing differently, and if it is, in what ways is it doing so? Doubts remain as to just how effective the plan and, yes, this new thinking at Citicorp, will be.

Among the most pressing problems to be addressed, Citicorp management (and, for that matter, a good many others throughout the financial community) generally agreed, was increasing the capital of the organization. The assessment is indeed accurate.

1
A Capital Problem

Dr. Paul Nadler, a keen observer of the banking scene (as well as professor of banking at Rutgers University), once said that having adequate capital is something most bankers consider akin to the human appendix. It is thought about only when it begins to cause trouble—or when the banking regulators bring up the topic.

Because of the volatility in the financial industry during the past decade or so and the rash of bank failures and near failures all around the world (but most significantly here in the United States), capital is a topic that has been increasingly raised by the regulators. After all, a bank's capital is supposed to ease the situation should a bank get in trouble. Such funds are a bastion against bad loans and even worse management. If the regulators determine that a bank's capital is insufficient, that institution may be required to raise additional capital, refrain from doing some kinds of banking business, or both.

Redefining Capital

Just what is bank capital? What is the meaning of these two words that are being tossed around so frequently during this final decade of the twentieth century?

Bank capital is basically defined as being composed of long-term debt and owners' equity. But, in practice, bank capital really is what the regulators say it is. And they have changed the definition—and the ground rules by which the banks must play—to encompass the element of risk that is included in much of what can be considered debt and equity. In so doing, the regulators have succeeded in making the definition of cap-

15

ital so complex and convoluted that many bankers themselves don't understand what it means anymore. For that matter, we sometimes wonder if the regulators understand their own rules.

Risk-based capital guidelines were agreed to in 1988 by the major international trading countries of the world, including the United States; in 1989 they were adopted as minimum standards for the U.S. banks by the federal banking regulatory agencies—the Federal Reserve, the Federal Deposit Insurance Corporation (FDIC), and the comptroller of the currency. These guidelines have been phased-in with stringent rules which have increased capital amounts over a period of years, with the final minimums required to be reached by the end of 1992.

Under these new guidelines, bank capital is divided into two groups, Tier 1 (Core capital) and Tier 2 (Supplementary capital). Tier 1 includes such items as common-stock equity, noncumulative perpetual preferred stock, and surplus (if any); Tier 2 includes loan loss reserves and cumulative preferred stock. By the end of 1992, banks must have total capital equal to 8 percent of risk-weighted assets, with at least half (4 percent) composed of Tier 1, or core capital. The problem for a good many U.S. banks, particularly large banks such as Citicorp, is that the new rules not only increase the minimum capital required from what had been 6 percent, they also redefine and place limits on the specific balance sheet items that can be included under the umbrella term "capital."

The Citi Line

In January of 1991, John Reed briefed a meeting of stock analysts and investors, taking stock of Citicorp's situation. On the matter of capital, he had this to say:

> Over the next two years, we want to become known as a strongly capitalized company. We feel it is important from the stockholders' point of view to strengthen our relative as well as absolute capital positions, and we have developed a plan by which to do so. Given current difficulties we may not hit every target in this plan exactly on schedule, but we do believe we can put together the necessary steps to achieve our capital goals, including a build-up through retained earnings.

Here is what the bank officially said in its annual report a year later about how it would achieve its objective of strengthening its capital base:

> The program to increase Citicorp's capital position involves adding $4 billion to $5 billion to the 1990 Tier 1 capital base. This is to be ac-

complished principally through retained earnings, but also includes selling non-strategic assets, managing the balance sheet, and raising external capital. The goal is to meet applicable regulatory guidelines by year-end 1992 and substantially exceed them in 1993. During 1991, important capital-building steps were taken:

- Tier 1 capital increased a net $541 million, and total Tier 1 and Tier 2 capital increased to $17.1 billion—more than any other U.S. bank.
- $1.25 billion in new preferred stock was sold to outside investors.
- Various asset sales had the equivalent effect of adding $1.2 billion to Tier 1 capital.
- Suspension of the common-stock dividend eliminated annual payments of almost $350 million.
- The Tier 1 capital ratio, calculated according to year-end 1992 guidelines, was raised to 3.7 percent from 3.3 percent.

Interestingly, and perhaps pertinently, in that statement Citicorp says its capital at the beginning of 1992 amounted to $17.1 billion—"more than that of any other U.S. bank."

Well, of course it is more than any other U.S. bank. With its assets at the end of 1991 nearly double the assets of its closest competitor (BankAmerica Corporation, the parent of the Bank of America), Citi's total capital would have to be substantially more. The big problem comes in the percentage of capital Citicorp actually has on hand. At year-end 1991, Citicorp's total capital ratio was 7.46 percent; BankAmerica, which in the late 1980s was nearly given up for dead, had a capital ratio of 10.8 percent.

The Parts Are Better Than the Whole. We have been talking about Citicorp as a whole, the holding company which is composed of Citibank and numerous other banking companies and subsidiary organizations. It is interesting to note that some of these subsidiaries are actually rather well capitalized, far better than the parent.

For example, in a discussion of bank ratings and the fact that they don't always take into account various organizational units, David C. Cates, the chairman of Washington-based Ferguson & Company and well-known analyst on bank performance, pointed out that Citibank South Dakota is a highly profitable, well-reserved, and well-capitalized bank. Moreover, he said, the South Dakota unit pays a "strong dividend to its parent for its debt service needs." However, Cates noted that Citibank, N.A., the flagship bank in the organization, "meets none of these desirable standards."

For that matter, capital has not always been a top priority at Citicorp. For years, during the salad days under Walter Wriston and right up to the beginning of the 1990s, Citi gained a reputation for running fast with only a thin edge of capital. But that was alright, so the reasoning went; the very size of the bank and the diversity of its activities allowed units to make up for losses incurred by other units. Unfortunately, this theory doesn't necessarily work when revenues drop and loans all across the board turn sour. It sure hasn't worked at Citicorp.

Reed, himself, has acknowledged that the concept is no longer valid. "For years, we felt the principal strength of the company was the diversification our earnings stream which would allow us to operate with thinner capital than could other banks," he said recently, speaking to a group of investment analysts, "—but it clearly is not enough, given the reaction in the marketplace." This was quite an admission—and quite a break from the philosophy of previous leaders of the organization, including Reed's mentor, Walter Wriston.

The riskiness of such a mode of operation simply caught up with Citicorp, long one of the most undercapitalized of major U.S. banks.

Raising External Capital

The seriousness and the urgency of Citicorp's capital deficiencies finally was brought home to John Reed during the autumn of 1990 when he had a lunch with Gerald Corrigan, president of the Federal Reserve Bank of New York. Corrigan, who is not known for his subtlety and on occasion can be almost brutally blunt, strongly urged that Citi take steps as soon as possible to improve its financial condition, its capital position in particular. The consequences of not acting upon Corrigan's suggestions with all deliberate speed did not have to be spelled out to Reed.

One obvious place to go would be to the equity market, a point that Reed alluded to in his talk to security analysts:

> It is also in our minds to turn to the marketplace to increase capital. We are concerned about the dilution that would be involved in going to the market in today's environment. We are sensitive to the fact that stockholders were not well treated by the market last year, and we do not want to aggravate the situation. On the other hand, we believe that to be seen as strengthening our capital in today's marketplace would generate a response that would, ultimately, reward stockholders. Accordingly, we believe that some dilution can be justified against the payoff from being seen as more strongly capitalized. Citicorp's senior management is well invested when you cut the dividend or dilute stockholders' equity because, frankly, we are doing it to ourselves.

The first evidence of Citicorp's willingness to take drastic measures to correct its capital situation was made in no uncertain terms when the sale of a special issue of preferred stock paying an exceptionally high dividend of 11 percent was announced by the bank in February of 1991. Actually, the sales effort had been put in motion several weeks earlier, so Reed must have had this in mind during his talk to the analysts.

The 11 percent dividend rate, well above the prime rate Citi was then charging its best customers, showed how desperate the bank was to add to its capital base. But not only was the rate a costly one for the bank, the issue was not being sold to an investor group or to several investors; it was being sold to one individual who would own a significant portion of the banking company.

The Saudi Sale

The individual purchaser, Prince Alwaleed Bin Talal Bin Abdulaziz Al Saud, a member of the royal family of Saudi Arabia [and not the one who is involved in the Bank of Commerce and Credit International (B.C.C.I.) scandal], already owned 4.9 percent of the bank's common stock, which he had quietly acquired in bits and pieces during the previous several months. The 11 percent rate on the newly issued preferred stock, incidentally, works out to be equal to a hefty pretax rate of 15 percent for a corporate investor.

As part of the purchase arrangement, the prince would be allowed to convert the preferred stock to common stock at a price of $16 per share. With the converted stock added to the common stock he already owned, that meant the prince could wind up owning over 14 percent of Citicorp. While all this may have been unsettling to some within the bank, the bottom line was that $590 million in additional—and much needed—capital would be coming into the bank.

What the Regulators Required

Even if the management of the bank were not overly concerned with the stock ownership aspects of the deal, the federal regulators were. There was a flurry of correspondence and meetings during February 1991 among representatives of the bank, Prince Alwaleed, and the Board of Governors of the Federal Reserve System.

U.S. banking regulations made it necessary for the bank to notify the Federal Reserve of the pending sale of sizable blocks of stock and get its approval. A meeting was held on February 18, 1991, between J. Virgil Mattingly, general counsel for the Board, and several people representing both Citicorp's and the purchaser's interests—Richard Poulson and Neal Petersen from the Washington law firm of Hogan & Hartson;

Faissal Fahad al-Talal, who represents the prince's interests in the United States; and John Roche and Carl Howard, lawyers representing Citicorp.

In a letter to Mattingly the next day confirming the points covered at the meeting, Mr. Poulson wrote, in part:

> As we discussed, HRH [His Royal Highness, the prince] currently owns individually 4.9 percent of the outstanding common stock of Citicorp. He proposes to acquire through a wholly owned single purpose corporation incorporated in the Netherlands, of which HRH will be the sole beneficial owner, nonvoting preferred shares of Citicorp convertible into an additional 9.9 percent of Citicorp's common stock. The corporation will engage in no activities other than holding the investment in Citicorp and will have no external debt. The funds utilized for the investment will be derived solely from HRH's personal resources.

For the board, Mattingly requested a statement of provisions pertaining to issues of control. In response as part of correspondence on February 20, 1991, Poulson sent a long list of commitments authorized by the prince. In summary, these stated that HRH would not, without the board's prior approval:

- Exercise or attempt to exercise a controlling influence over the management or policies of Citicorp or any depository subsidiary.
- Have or seek to have any employees or representatives serve as an officer, agent, or employee of Citicorp.
- Take any action causing Citicorp or any of its depository subsidiaries to become a subsidiary of the Company or any other affiliate of HRH.
- Acquire or obtain shares that would cause the combined interest of HRH the Company, other affiliates of HRH, and any officers or directors to equal or exceed 25 percent of the outstanding voting shares of Citicorp.
- Propose a director or slate of directors in opposition to a nominee or slate of nominees proposed by the management or board of Citicorp.
- Attempt to influence the dividend policies or practices of Citicorp.
- Attempt to influence the loan and credit decisions or policies of Citicorp, the pricing of services, any personnel decision, the location of any offices, except that HRH will be permitted to communicate his view to the board and vote his securities in any manner consistent with these commitments.

The commitments also stated that the prince would not dispose or threaten to dispose of his Citicorp shares in a manner requiring a specific action or nonaction on the part of the institution. However, he would be permitted to establish and maintain deposit accounts with the bank, but only to an aggregate balance of $500,000.

In another letter to Mattingly on February 20 following a telephone conversation with the Fed official, Poulson stated that the funds for the investment in the convertible preferred stock were solely the funds of the prince and:

- Were not borrowed
- Did not come from any bank in which the prince had an ownership interest
- Did not come from any company in which the prince had an interest

That same correspondence also stated that "The basis for HRH's desire to have an extended period of time in which to dispose of his 4.9 percent common stock holding is that he wishes to make the decision to sell on an economic basis, rather than on a forced sell basis."

The actual purchase agreement for the stock, dated February 21, 1991, was 29 pages long.

One year later, almost to the day, Prince Alwaleed notified the Federal Reserve Board that he intended to hold onto his Citicorp stock and, in fact, would not be selling the 4.9 percent of common stock he owned. He also affirmed that he had no plans to control a seat on the board or to increase his holdings beyond 24.9 percent.

If he did convert his preferred stock to common stock, the prince would own approximately 14 percent of the Citicorp common stock, making him by far the largest single stockholder in the company. It should be pointed out that, according to the provisions of the preferred stock issue, the Saudi prince cannot convert the preferred stock to common stock for five years from the date of the sale, or until February 1996. (At present, Wellington Management Company, Boston, owns 8.05 percent of Citicorp common stock, the only person or group owning more than 5 percent of any class of the organization's voting securities.)

How the Deal With the Prince Came About

As noted earlier, the prince had a definite interest in Citicorp and had been buying a lot of common stock, although his specific reasons have never been divulged, other than the fact that he did so for "investment purposes." Be that as it may, he wanted to increase his investment and told his agent, Faissal Fahad, of this interest.

Fahad discussed the matter with an old friend of his, Alphonso Christian, a partner with the Washington law firm of Hogan & Hartson.

Christian, who has impeccable connections in the nation's capital (where the right connections are almost everything), mentioned the matter to a principal of the Carlyle Group, a relatively young merger and acquisition firm, also based in Washington. While it has not had much of a track record in the investment business, its members do have excellent (and bipartisan) Washington connections. These principals include David M. Rubenstein, who was a domestic policy adviser for President Jimmy Carter; Frank Carlucci, secretary of defense in the Reagan administration; and Fred Malek, a close associate of President Bush. Malek subsequently took a leave of absence from the firm to work on Bush's 1992 presidential campaign.

A meeting was arranged between Faissal Fahad and the Carlyle people. The firm was given the opportunity to handle the transaction because of the reputation of the group's members and not, as previously noted, because of its experience. It also didn't hurt that Carlyle only charged the prince a reported $50,000 to arrange the deal—which is not more than a drop in the bucket in what eventually turned out to be more than a half-billion-dollar transaction. Actually, it is reported that the Carlyle people wound up getting much, much more compensation, but how much more, no one is willing to say.

However, it is understood that Citicorp paid the additional money, not the prince. This is yet another indication of how eager Citicorp was to make the sale.

An Even Bigger Sale

Just two weeks after the prince bought his stock in March of 1991, $600 million more of the newly issued preferred stock was sold to a group of a little more than three dozen institutional investors.

Those investors, however, did not get quite as good a deal as Prince Alwaleed; their dividend is 10¾ percent, compared to his 11 percent. Also, the price for converting the preferred stock to common stock was pegged at $18.25 per share; the prince can convert his at $16. Still, the sale represented a lucrative investment for the group and another costly arrangement for acquiring additional capital for Citicorp. Stephen L. Norris, one of the Carlyle partners and the man who actually managed the sale with the prince for the Carlyle Group, reiterated the fact that the prince actually had the better deal—$85 million better, to be more precise.

Morgan Stanley & Company handled this latter deal, one that began at $500 million. However, because there was so much investor interest in the sale, the amount of stock offered and sold was raised to $600 million. Morgan Stanley had an option on an additional 15 percent to sell to the investors on the same terms. An additional 10 percent, $60 million, eventually was added to the sale, for a total of $660 million.

Apparently the sale to the Saudi prince served, in part, as an inducement to attract other investors, which, of course, it did. The earlier sale demonstrated to those investors that Citicorp was serious about raising the capital it needed so much—and willing to pay for it in the process. By so doing, Citicorp also increased the investors' confidence in the viability of the banking company. Certainly, adding $1.25 billion in new capital over the space of two weeks or so was an exceptional event and a mark of the respect Citicorp still commands in the world financial marketplace.

The problem is there aren't too many people (or groups of people) with that kind of money available to them who also do not want (or profess not to want) to exercise some kind of control over their purchase.

However, John Reed was so pleased that the second sale had actually come off that he announced it almost before the ink was dry on the agreement. The announcement was made at a rare (for him) news conference which he held March 6, 1991, while on a trip to Buenos Aires. "We are basically getting the first step of this [capital-raising] program completed and we are very pleased with it," Reed told Reuters.

The fact remains that his capital-raising program has proven to be extremely expensive. Just how expensive is demonstrated by the fact that in the second quarter of 1991, the dividends paid out on the preferred stock amounted to *more* than Citicorp's earnings for the period.

Other Equity Issues

Pleased as Citicorp was with those two big sales, it still needed more capital, much more.

Unfortunately, earnings reported in each quarter of 1991 showed substantial drops from the year-ago period, capped by a huge loss of nearly $900 million in the third quarter—the largest quarterly loss since 1987 when the bank added $5 billion to its reserves against LDC loans. Obviously, this was not the time to raise capital through equity sales. Even if Citicorp tried, the very good possibility of poor response to an offer would have had an additional negative impact on the banking company. There was enough bad news in 1991 without adding to it.

However, confidence in Citicorp seemed to improve during the early months of 1992. There were indications that the bank was, in fact, seriously addressing its troubles and was getting closer to the government-mandated capital minimums. Other banks, it seemed, were tapping strong investor demand with stock offerings, so why not Citicorp? Consequently, in mid-March, it decided to sell $150 million in preferred stock, the first offering in over a year. The stock was marketed with a dividend rate of 9.05 percent, well below the rate given to the prince and to the group of institutional investors in 1991. It was not expected that the latest stock sale would add more than 0.1 percent to the bank's capital position.

As soon as the offering was made public, however, Standard & Poor's (S&P) announced that it was lowering the rating on Citicorp preferred stock, including the new issue, from BBB to BBB−. This followed a move during the fall of 1991 by the firm to downgrade Citi's debt and preferred stock. In its latest announcement, S&P noted both the high fixed cost of the preferred stock and the fact that the company had been relying so heavily on this kind of stock to improve its capital position.

"Coverage will remain thin, as the company's substantial loan quality problems will likely dampen earnings over the intermediate term," the S&P announcement read, which could only be described as an understatement. It added that the ratings could drop more if earnings continued low or nonexistent because of chronic loan problems.

Moody's Investors Service, it should be pointed out, had already rated Citicorp preferred stock slightly lower than the new S&P rating. Its rating is Ba-1, which is considered just below investment grade.

Will the lower ratings hurt additional equity offerings during the balance of 1992? Perhaps not, but they are hardly likely to help.

Interestingly, the *American Banker* noted in the spring that Citicorp's chief financial officer, Thomas Jones, indicated that there would be no common-stock issues during the balance of 1992. However, a number of analysts believed there would be a stock issue before the end of 1992. Jones was correct. No stock issues occurred during the balance of 1992.

Preferred for Sale

As it turned out, there has been an offering of 42 million shares of preferred stock, with a total market value of $650 million. The offering was announced in August 1991, and to attract investors, the interest rates range from 7.75 to 8.25 percent. These rates are much higher than current bank certificates of deposit or Treasury notes. Because the shares can be converted to common stock, they are called preferred equity redemption cumulative share (or PERCS).

The prospectus, issued on October 6, 1992, also included statements relating to the fact that Citibank does not currently meet the numerical capital standards applicable to "well-capitalized" institutions. However, it noted, Citicorp had, as of June 30, 1991, combined Tier 1 and Tier 2 capital of $18.5 billion, which amounts to 8.50 percent of risk-adjusted assets.

In the same prospectus, details were given about a memorandum of understanding executed on February 19, 1992, with the Federal Reserve Bank of New York and the Office of the Comptroller of the Currency (OCC). Some of the information in the memorandum had already been made public, but the following statement was hardly encouraging for investors:

> The memorandum of understanding provides that Citicorp will not transfer, bid for, acquire, or enter into agreements to acquire, significant bank or nonbank entities or asset or liability portfolios or expand its consolidated assets or activities without first consulting with the Reserve Bank and the OCC.

Giant Asset Sale Now Going On

Fortunately for Citicorp, there have been other routes to be taken to raise capital besides selling stock. It could sell some of its noncore banking business interests, both good and bad. The sale of the good would, of course, command attractive prices, and the sale of the bad would get rid of those units that had contributed negatively to the bottom line. Of course, selling the good assets means losing the profits that they generate. Oh, well; you can't have everything. So Citi has been doing a lot of asset selling during the past couple of years, though not as much as it would like to have done (or it hopes to do in future months and years).

The banking company has had some major successes in its asset sales. It estimates that 1991 sales had the effect of adding $1.2 billion to its Tier 1 capital. On the other hand, some of the sales were not all that successful, and other sales have not come off.

While the following list of Citi's asset sales is not all-inclusive, it does provide a representative picture of the kind of items the bank has been trying to sell in order to add to its capital base.

1. *Saudi American Bank (SAMBA).*   Citi sold 25 percent of its ownership in SAMBA, which it helped to found in 1980. It still retains a 30 percent interest in the bank, and the plans are to continue its management of the organization. The Riyadh-based bank has been extremely successful, earning $200 million in 1991. Citicorp's gain on the sale was $203 million.

2. *Ambac.*   A municipal bond insurance subsidiary, Ambac, Inc., was also founded by Citicorp. The insurer has proven to be a winner, with 1990 profits of $105 million. The sale was consummated in two parts. The first, in mid-1991, was not all that successful. At a selling

price of $20 per share, the sale raised $352 million in capital. But this was about 30 percent less than the bank wanted, and it actually took a loss of nearly $50 million, after taxes, fees, and other charges. Citi fared far better with the sale of the remaining stake in Ambac in early 1992. The stock was sold at $31.75 a share and raised a total of $550 million. The net profit on the two-part sale was approximately $100 million.

Although Ambac was a highly profitable subsidiary, its stock had appreciated and it was immensely salable. Moreover, as a matter of policy, Citicorp had decided to sell as many of its noncore businesses as possible. In other words, Ambac was expendable.

3. *Lynch, Jones & Ryan.* The brokerage firm, Lynch, Jones & Ryan, was sold in December 1991 for around $15 million. That's only a drop in the Citicorp capital bucket, but it's another illustration of the bank's efforts to sell noncore business, large and small.

4. *Capital Markets Assurance Corporation (CapMac).* This subsidiary provided insurance for the issuers of asset-backed securities. Over the years, it had been highly profitable, earning $13 million on sales of $32 million in 1991. The unit was nearly sold in the autumn of 1991 to the Financial Guaranty Insurance Company, but the deal fell through. In June 1992, CapMac was sold to a group of investors including CapMac's management; Dillon Read's Saratoga Partners II, L.P.; an investment group comprising members of the William Rockefeller family; and a number of other investors. Citicorp did not announce the terms of the sale, only stating that "the sale is part of Citicorp's continuing program to strengthen its ratios by selling nonstrategic businesses."

5. *Citibank Italia.* This Citicorp unit has 50 branches in southern Italy. It was sold to Banco Ambrosiano Veneto, Italy's largest private bank, for $273 million. The sale produced the net effect of raising Citi's capital by $125 million. This was one response to the substantial losses the bank has been experiencing in parts of its global business recently; unfortunately, those losses had not been occurring at Citibank Italia. And Citi is holding on to a variety of other banking businesses in Italy for the time being.

6. *Citicorp Establishment Services.* The third-largest processor of merchant credit card business in the country has been the object of rumors for months. Finally, at the end of June 1992, following several public denials, Citicorp sold the unit to Welsh, Carson, Anderson & Stowe, a venture capital company that specializes in transaction-processing companies. The sale was expected to bring in at least $150 million and, in fact, it was actually sold for $175 million. This figure could be classified as almost total profit, since the assets have long been fully depreciated.

Other banking companies have been getting out of the merchant processing business, including Chase, First Chicago, and Manufacturers Hanover, so such a sale is hardly unprecedented.

Another reason that a sale may have been decided upon was the less-than-favorable publicity the subsidiary gained in the autumn of 1991 when it was reported that several of its top executives were charged with overstating revenues. (More details of this can be found in Chapter 11.)

7. *Assets From Loan Defaults.* A number of real estate holdings, which Citicorp took when loans were defaulted, have been sold. These and other similarly gained assets will be discussed in the following chapter.

Sales and Rumors of Sales

It is widely known that Citicorp would dearly love to unload Quotron, which has never made money since it was acquired in 1986. Not only has this supplier of stock quotations lost money, considerable amounts of funds have been poured into the subsidiary to make it more competitive and to restructure the unit, which includes cutting back on the number of employees. So far, nothing seems to have worked. Because of all that, and because the stock quote company has such strong competition, the unit may well remain a drag on earnings for years to come.

According to Citicorp officials, there are as many as a dozen other business units that may be sold. John Reed confirmed this fact but he would not disclose which units had the potential to be sold because, he said, that might reduce the price bidders would be willing to pay. He did say that Citi was looking "at asset utilizations and the scope of our business with a fine-tooth comb."

The problem with selling assets is that, in most cases, the units that can be profitably sold are the ones that have been profitable themselves. When you are trying to do everything possible to increase earnings—or simply to get out of the red—getting rid of assets that generate profits makes the overall objective just that much more difficult to reach. A bank that sells its profitable assets, critics point out, is a bank that is selling its future. But what else can a company in trouble do? Sometimes there just is no other choice.

The Questions Remain

In his report made at the bank's annual meeting in April 1992 concerning first-quarter results, John Reed announced that Citicorp had added

$1.0 billion to its capital. This brought its total capital ratio to 8.12 percent, with Tier 1 capital at 4.06 percent, slightly above the minimums required at the end of 1992.

Remembering what had happened in 1991, there was some concern that the ratios might not hold throughout the year. However, in reporting its third-quarter earnings for 1992, the company said that total regulatory capital stood at $18.7 billion, or 8.50 percent of risk-based assets, with the Tier 1 capital ratio at 4.25 percent. Not only did this exceed the minimums, Citicorp pointed out that its sale of $1 billion of conversion preferred stock (PERCS), which closed late in October 1992, would increase the Tier 1 capital ratio by about 25 basis points and have the effect of building total regulatory capital to approximately $20 billion.

But even with this performance, the capital levels at Citicorp remain below the levels at many of the other major banks in New York and elsewhere in the country. Most of these banks, such as Chemical and Chase, which also haven't been performing all that well in recent years, have Tier 1 capital around the 6 percent level. That fact alone makes them more competitive and places Citi at a potential and possibly even substantial disadvantage.

During the early months of 1992, there was a resurgence of positive thinking about Citicorp by several bank stock analysts, in large measure, apparently, because of its capital-raising efforts. At the same time, other analysts pointed out, moving from 4 to 6 percent will be extremely difficult, if not impossible, for Citi to do for at least a few years. When Citi started making its moves on capital at the beginning of 1991, John Reed announced that he would seek an additional $5 billion in fresh capital. Charles Peabody, of Kidder Peabody and a frequent critic of both Reed and his bank, estimated that Citicorp would actually need as much as $7 billion in new capital. If that is true, it is hard to see where the additional money will come from; chances are, the bank cannot get it.

Certainly, any profits that are generated and that can be retained will help the capital situation. And, it would seem that Reed is counting on this. "We're going to earn our way there," he says.

The earnings for the first quarter of 1992 were reported at $0.37 per share, compared to $0.17 per share in 1991. But after taking into account an accounting change on the investments of its venture capital subsidiaries, we can calculate the 1991 first-quarter earnings to have amounted to $1.48 per share. No matter how one wants to deal with the figures, the results show just how far Citicorp has to travel before earnings will add in any substantive way to its capital base. Of course, as long as its loan portfolio remains in such awful shape, particularly its real estate loans, the outlook for Citicorp is hardly encouraging (see Chapter 2).

Dividends have been suspended since the third quarter of 1991. It's anyone's guess when they will be restored. But it won't be long before stockholders will want to share in the profits, if any. On the other hand, if profits are low and remain weak, investors will shy away from Citicorp as a viable bank stock.

So, although Citicorp's capital situation is measurably better at the end of the first two quarters of 1992 than it was in 1991 or 1990, it still is not good. How much better it may be in 1993 is anybody's guess.

In the meantime, the organization's stature remains diminished and the competition is getting ever closer to the once great Citicorp.

2
Loan Portfolios Gone Bad

After great effort in building capital—and sales of some of its money-making subsidiaries—Citicorp ended 1992 above the capital minimums mandated by the regulatory authorities.

However, as pointed out in the preceding chapter, other banks that also have been experiencing problems of late have been able to do far better in exceeding those capital requirements. One result of this fact is that Citicorp is still in the process of trying to build its capital base and is still selling some of its subsidiaries.

Another aspect of the Citicorp picture, and perhaps just as important as capital at the beginning of 1993, is its loan portfolio. It was just awful at the end of 1991 and did not improve all that much during 1992. In fact, it is the one major factor that continues to cloud the outlook for Citicorp.

The question, then, is just how dreadful will the loan portfolio be?

In fact, a recent and close examination of all segments of the portfolio indicates that things are continuing to move from bad to not quite as bad. Unfortunately, this less-than-sparkling performance is occurring while much of the rest of the banking community is on the rebound. No wonder details on its loan picture are usually relegated to deep within the financial information section pages of Citicorp's annual reports.

The Consumer Loan Picture

Citi has placed a lot of those chips Walter Wriston was talking about in the consumer lending business. For a while, the investment paid off quite handsomely; in fact, the consumer business has remained one of the few consistently bright spots during John Reed's tenure.

There was a brief slide in 1985, John Reed's first full year as chairman, and a time when the economy was doing rather well. Part of the problem, bank officials say, was due to the aggressive marketing of credit cards; they point out that such new accounts have credit losses three times the ongoing average. The marketing efforts did pay off by bringing in 3 million new accounts for the second year in a row.

Consumer loan losses increased substantially in 1985 over 1984, to a total of $585 million, net of recoveries. Reserves for possible credit losses were also increased to approximately double the 1984 figure. But the amount allotted to the individual bank ("individual bank" being Citicorp lingo, or "Citi-ese," for its consumer banking business) was $285 million, which amounted to only 0.50 percent of the consumer loan portfolio—a figure woefully low by almost any prudent banker's standard. For some reason or another, Citicorp management seemed unable to face the fact that consumer loans could go bad and those losses ought to be adequately covered.

In 1986, the consumer lending business increased, as did profits, with Citi moving into five new markets nationally. Although profits continued to increase, so did loan losses, nearly doubling the year-earlier figures. In 1987, consumer lending did well, and net write-offs as a percentage of average outstandings declined to 1.43 percent; this was down from 1.56 percent in the previous year. This trend continued through 1988 and 1989 and into 1990. And so did the reluctance to put aside the kinds of reserves demanded by these loan losses.

It was at that point that the economic downturn in the United States and in some other parts of the world began to have an impact on Citicorp's consumer loan portfolio. The individual bank as a whole continued to show a profit, even in 1991. But loan write-offs rose dramatically, as did (finally) the provisions for loan losses. Also, as might be expected, total consumer loan volume dropped, both in 1990 and 1991, after gains were registered continuously through most of the 1980s.

More specifically, in 1991, revenues were down and credit costs were up. The provision for loan losses was increased by about a third, and net income dropped 39 percent from the 1990 figure. The allowance for consumer credit losses was 1.24 percent of year-end loans, compared with 0.98 percent the previous year. The amount was increased to 1.38 percent at the end of the second quarter of 1992. But even that figure still seems low when you consider the residual effects of the recession that still is plaguing us. Even if the economy continues its painfully slow recovery, the allowance won't be setting any records. In the face of this sluggish movement, it would seem that a relatively low allowance for consumer loan losses won't do much more than drag out the grief that much longer.

The consumer loan delinquency ratio at Citicorp went from 3.0 percent in 1989 to 4.8 percent in 1991. Many of the delinquencies—loans 90 days or more past due—were in household mortgages. In its 1991 annual report, Citicorp cautioned that the rate could increase, depending upon economic conditions. This proved to be accurate; the first quarter of 1992 showed an increase in total consumer 90-day delinquencies of $200 million, to $4.6 billion at the end of the quarter. As already noted, with a less-than-robust economy, delinquencies are apt to increase during a good part of this year.

To pump up its slowing credit card business, Citi followed the lead of American Express and lowered some of its rates. "About time," many customers could be heard saying, since the cost of money has been dropping while credit card rates have stayed high. Because American Express only lowered the rates on its Optima card, the Citicorp move will have far greater impact, and it wasn't long before other banks announced similar reductions.

This Citicorp effort is a calculated risk on the part of the bank. Many observers of the credit card business believe the market is close to being saturated. Obviously, Citi hopes to attract customers from other banks and, at the same time, encourage their good customers to buy more, thereby increasing the overall credit card take and making up for any decline in the interest rate. Of course, it will help immeasurably if the economy develops some steam.

Overall, consumer lending has been a Godsend to Citicorp, and a fading recession should be welcome. However, that situation may not be all that bright if in a recovering economy Citicorp finds itself facing bigger and better competitors than it faced before the downturn.

Cross-Border Loans

"Cross Border" is another example of Citi-ese. The phrase refers to funds invested or loaned across national borders. While most of the loans overseas do not cause out-of-the-ordinary problems, loans to the developing countries have done so—and continue to do so.

Because of the policies of Walter Wriston and others under his direction, Citicorp has had a significant exposure in less-developed country (LDC) loans. These can be good loans when a country is, in fact, developing and improving its economic position. But when things go the other way, and the governments are unstable, the result can be a significant drag on earnings.

This poor performance is exactly what happened at Citicorp (and at many other banks that had followed Citicorp's lead into this volatile lending market) during the mid-1980s. The deterioration of this loan portfolio escalated after Wriston left the scene.

The international debt problem, by general consensus, dates back to August 1982. Over the years, there were attempts to get things back on track, including the Baker initiative (named after then–Secretary of the Treasury James Baker) in 1985, in which countries were encouraged to utilize free-market solutions to their financial woes. On balance, not much came of that initiative—or anything else, for that matter.

However, at the end of 1986, Citicorp tried to put the best possible spin on this deteriorating situation. It stated in its annual report that "the key question is whether the developing countries have the political will to continue to take the steps needed for stable growth. The evidence to date is, by and large, that they do."

At year-end 1986, Citicorp had "outstandings to refinancing countries" (another Citi-ese term for LDC loans) amounting to a total of $14.9 billion. The countries involved included Brazil and Mexico, where Citi's cross-border and currency outstandings in each country exceeded 1 percent of the bank's total assets. Other countries (where the outstandings were under ¾ of 1 percent of assets—a not-inconsiderable amount) included Argentina, the Philippines, and Venezuela.

In February 1987, Brazil announced that it was suspending the repayment of interest on intermediate- and long-term public- and private-sector foreign currency obligations to banks. Because of this interest payment suspension, Citicorp acted decisively, placing $3.8 billion of its intermediate- and long-term outstandings on a cash basis. That move reduced the bank's after-tax earnings by $200 million for 1987.

Two months later, in April, some $9.6 billion of medium-term public- and private-sector debt came due under a restructuring agreement that had been signed in 1986. The government of Brazil sent a telex to its creditor banks requesting them to extend the maturity of the debt to July 15, 1988. Also, the Central Bank of Brazil asked the banks to accept interim measures for the maturities of other public- and private-sector debt that was falling due during 1987 and the first half of 1988.

In addition, the other refinancing countries were experiencing problems, and there was an obvious need for restructuring of their debt, as well.

The situation became so tenuous that in May 1987 Citicorp, under the direction of John Reed, announced that it was increasing its reserves by $3.0 billion, reflecting its increased concern over the risk of its loans to developing countries. Among other things, this move, the bank stated, "would allow it greater flexibility in managing its portfolio, for example, by participating actively in debt trading and debt/equity conversions." This flexibility apparently worked, because the bank was able to reduce its cross-border exposure to refinancing countries by $1.3 billion by the end of 1987. However, that still left Citicorp's exposure in those nations at a whopping $13.3 billion.

Adding to its reserves by such a huge amount negated what would otherwise have been a good year for Citicorp. As a result, it ended 1987 with a loss of $1.182 billion, the largest by far in its history.

At the same time, John Reed received high marks for taking the kind of hit he did and facing up to the ongoing international debt problem. Many other banks followed his lead, although not all, and most of those that did were not particularly happy with the situation or with the actions they felt were forced upon them. It may have been Reed's finest hour.

The LDC Problems Linger On

Outstanding loans to refinancing countries continued to depress Citicorp earnings in 1988, with more loans put on a cash basis, though not nearly to the extent that the 1987 actions caused. In 1989, because both Argentina and Brazil were not paying interest on their debts, the bank increased its reserves by another $1 billion. This resulted in a loss of $1.151 billion, in this segment of the business, compared to net income of $278 million in 1988. And even with average assets reduced to $11 billion, the exposure remained high.

Brazil continued to be a thorn in Citicorp's side. At the end of 1990, the total Brazilian debt in arrears approximated $8 billion, including half a billion dollars due but unpaid to Citi. In the second quarter of 1990, the bank wrote off $631 million of its medium- and long-term exposure to Brazil. The write-off reduced the carrying value of the affected outstanding loans by 20 percent. At the end of the year, Citicorp was carrying its $2.1 billion in medium- and long-term outstandings on a cash basis. This move reduced the bank's earnings by 313 million pretax dollars. The experience with Argentina hasn't been much better, except that the bank's exposure there has been far less than in Brazil. New and previous write-offs, which were charged against the portion of Citi's allowance for possible credit losses attributable to the refinancing portfolio, reduced the carrying value of the outstandings affected to about 40 percent of par value.

Brazil kept on causing problems for Citicorp in 1991, although an agreement was signed with all of the country's creditor banks on settling its arrearages. Still, Citi continues to carry almost all of Brazil's $1.2 billion in medium- and long-term outstandings on a cash basis. And the bank charged new write-offs of $1.4 billion on its Brazilian outstandings. This reduced the carrying value of the medium- and long-term outstanding loans to an average of 37 percent of face value.

More recently, during the spring of 1992, Argentina and its foreign bank creditors, including Citicorp, reached a debt accord that could help to close the door on the decade-long Latin American debt crisis. In fact, William H. Rhodes, Citi vice chairman and its resident expert on the refinancing countries' loan problems, was the chief negotiator for the banks.

The cross-border portfolio had net income of $122 million in the first quarter of 1992, compared with $178 million in the fourth quarter of 1991 and a loss of $30 million during the first three months of 1991. Citi is not out of the woods yet, but the last of the trees is in sight.

Clearly, the loans to developing nations, particularly to the countries in Latin America already mentioned, proved to be costly for Citicorp. The exposure now has been reduced significantly, although the cost has been substantial, to say the least. One can only imagine what the bank's profits would have been without this drag on earnings over the past decade.

Awash in Bad Commercial Loans

Where Citicorp has gotten in deepest trouble in recent years has been with its commercial loan portfolio, and its real estate loans, in particular.

Commercial loans began turning sour in a big way in 1985. While the institutional bank (Citi-ese for its corporate business activities, as well as for business with other countries) made money that year, the amount was 14 percent less than in 1984. As the bank described the situation, "Net commercial loan write-offs were $377 million, or 65 basis points of the full-year average commercial loan portfolio, an increase of $156 million, or 27 basis points, over last year's level. Over the past 10 years, net write-offs as a percentage of the commercial loan portfolio have averaged 35 basis points...."

The years 1986 to 1989 were relatively stable for Citicorp's commercial lending business; the volume increased and so did its reserves for bad loans. However, there were increasing signs of trouble with real estate loans, mostly in the United States.

The other news in 1989 is that Citicorp changed its nomenclature for the institutional bank; the new phrase used to describe its business is "global finance." For that matter, the phrase "institutional bank" has been replaced by the new term, "global consumer." The idea, of course, is to underscore Citicorp as a worldwide financial institution. The company's international nature is hard to dispute; it seems to be getting more global all the time. After all, the largest single stockholder is from Saudi Arabia. And, as we shall see in the following chapter, the management of the bank is gaining a decidedly international flavor.

New Terminology, New Losses

The advent of 1990 saw a definite turn for the worse in the lending fortunes of Citicorp.

The global finance operations were divided into two groups with new names. For example, 1990 was the year JENA found its way into Citicorp's lexicology. JENA stands for Japan, Europe, and North America, except the grouping also includes Australia and New Zealand. The other group is called International Banking and Finance, which includes business in the developing countries, and the local franchises and presence in the countries of Latin America, Asia, eastern Europe, the Middle East, and Africa.

No matter what the name, JENA did not do well in 1990. It recorded a loss of $299 million, which is quite a step down from the net income of $614 million recorded in the previous year. This loss was properly blamed on problems in the U.S. real estate and leveraged-finance markets, plus economic troubles in Australia. Revenue growth was essentially flat, while credit costs soared (from $318 million in 1989 to $1.446 billion in 1990). These costs included a half-billion-dollar increase in the commercial loan loss allowance, a big jump in net write-offs, the cost of carrying nonperforming assets, and OREO (Other Real Estate Owned) expenses. But, as they say, that's how the cookie crumbles.

Cash basis and renegotiated loans amounted to $4.9 billion at the end of 1990, more than doubling during the year. OREO totaled $1.3 billion, an increase of $1 billion during the year. Another trouble spot was the category of "highly leveraged transactions," which is discussed in detail below.

Worse Gets "Worser"

Perhaps it's understandable to put the best possible light on a bad situation. In Citicorp's annual report for 1991, John Reed writes that "Each of our core businesses—Consumer [what happened to global consumer?], Global Finance International, and Global Finance JENA, excluding troubled portfolios—remained sound, together earning $1.5 billion in 1991."

Obviously, there are some portfolios in JENA that are not troubled, but the fact is that JENA had a loss of $1.019 billion in 1991. That compares with a loss of $275 million in 1990.

The U.S. portfolio was particularly hard hit in 1991, and Citicorp admits it. This portfolio is composed primarily of commercial and industrial loans, mortgage and real estate loans, plus smaller amounts of loans to financial institutions and lease financing receivables.

Here's what the bank had to say in its 1991 annual report about its U.S. portfolio:

> Net credit losses in 1991 were substantial—$941 million, or 3.21 percent of average loans, up from $431 million, or 1.39 percent of average loans in 1990. Net credit losses included a $171 million write-off on exposure to First Capital Holdings, Inc. Net credit losses in U.S. commercial real estate lending increased substantially in 1991 to $511 million, up from $228 million in 1990, and are expected to increase further in 1992 as a result of slower, but continued, erosion of real estate values. Net credit losses decreased in U.S. leveraged acquisition finance activities to $137 million in 1991 from $162 million in 1990.

Apparently Citicorp's economic forecasters are not much better than economic forecasters generally. In its 1990 annual report, the bank stated that it expects, "over the next 12 to 18 months, its net credit losses on U.S. commercial loans will be in the range of 1.5 percent to 2.5 percent of the 1990 average commercial loans." The 1991 net credit losses were 3.21 percent of average loans.

It should be noted that in the 1991 report, the bank states that it expects that its net credit losses on U.S. commercial loans will range from 3.5 percent to 4.5 percent of the 1991 average commercial loans. For the sake of Citicorp, it is hoped that this prediction is more on target and the results are not worse.

A Deteriorating Real Estate Portfolio

The stark reality of the real estate lending problems at Citicorp is evident in this description of the situation given by the bank in the 1991 annual report:

> U.S. commercial real estate exposure at year-end 1991 was $18.6 billion, down $3.5 billion from a year ago. Citicorp has continued to reduce its U.S. commercial real estate exposure through maturities, paydowns, cancellations, negotiated reductions in unfunded commitments, write-offs, and write-downs. Cash payoffs and paydowns represent the largest component of the $3.5 million reduction.
>
> The portfolio is well diversified, both geographically and by project type, with office, retail, and residential comprising 35%, 21%,

and 15%, respectively. These sectors experienced continued deterioration in 1991, with increases in nonperforming assets of $910 million, $266 million, and $245 million, respectively. Write-offs were concentrated in the office and residential sectors, together comprising 60 percent of the total.

Vacancy rates in commercial office space remain high in many metropolitan areas; rents and, correspondingly, asset values have declined. This phenomenon, which is cyclical, is also evident in the residential sector and across the portfolio in varying degrees and has led to increases in nonperforming assets, net write-offs, and OREO write-downs. The severity of the downturn, however, varies greatly by region.

Net OREO write-downs for the year were $157 million, up $135 million from 1990, concentrated in office buildings ($81 million) and land ($33 million). Geographically, OREO write-downs were highest in the Southeast ($40 million), New England ($35 million), and the Mid-Atlantic ($32 million).

Clearly, Citicorp's real estate loans will continue to cause problems for some time.

The Tale of the Trump

One rather prominent example of Citicorp's troubles is with the loans it has made to Donald Trump. It seems obvious that Trump overextended himself, but why did Citicorp (and other) banks allow this to happen? Didn't they have access to the figures? And if they did, why were they ignored?

In a listing of Trump's woes by *Business Week*, over the past year or so, the Donald has given up the Trump Shuttle, Trump Palace Apartments, and his stock in Alexander's Department Store, with a total market value of about $360 million. In each of those holdings, Citicorp was the recipient of the deal or the lead lender in a syndicate of banks. Trump has also given up a number of other assets for which different banks took the lead, with Citicorp as a player. In addition, Citicorp now controls 49 percent of New York's Plaza Hotel. This could be a valuable piece of property for Citicorp if the bank waits long enough for the recovery and the fortunes of the Plaza to be turned around. But right now, the Plaza represents nearly $200 million of Citicorp money that is not doing the bank much good.

In some ways, the Alexander story is the saddest. In 1992, this 64-year-old retail chain filed for chapter 11 bankruptcy and closed its 11 remaining stores. When Trump was in his glory days during the mid-1980s, he noticed that Alexander's had great locations and valuable real estate properties and attempted to take control of the company. Not only didn't that work out, the stores began to lose money and Trump passed along his 27 percent stake in the company to Citicorp as part of a debt-restructuring agreement. Now Citi is hoping it can recover something from the real estate. But will the properties sell, and if they do, when will they be sold and for how much? If there is one thing Citi doesn't need right at the present time, it is more real estate that the bank can't move.

Leveraged Acquisition Finance Activities

Citicorp has been heavily involved in the financing of leveraged buyouts. According to Citi, these activities include client transactions for the acquisition, leveraged recapitalization, and management buyout of commercial and/or asset values. In addition to financing and distributing loans, the bank evaluates and structures transactions.

Because of the economic downturn, the bank's senior leveraged finance loans on a cash basis and net credit write-offs increased over the levels reached in 1990. As of year-end 1991, Citi was the senior creditor for some $3.7 billion in leveraged finance loans in the United States. This compares with $5.0 billion in 1990. The bank explains the decrease as primarily the result of repayments. However, it also is due to delistings, loans, sales, and write-offs. This business has decreased substantially because of the economic climate. At the end of 1991, Citicorp had outstanding loans to about 135 obligors representing 25 industries; at year-end 1990, there were 170 obligors and 30 industries. The two largest industries were media and entertainment ($0.9 billion at the end of 1991) and retail/wholesale ($0.6 billion).

Similar leveraged finance activities are conducted by Citicorp in six other countries, with outstanding loans of approximately $1.2 billion; the total was $2.2 billion in eight countries at the end of 1990.

Cash basis and renegotiated commercial loans, excluding those in the refinancing portfolio (those LDC loans) totaled $5.712 billion in 1991, up from $5.179 million in 1990. At the end of 1991, only $1.8 billion of those cash-basis loans were either current or overdue by less than 90 days. Included in this amount were $1.5 billion in real estate loans.

Is the Worst Yet to Come?

At the annual meeting in April 1992, John Reed said, "Our customer franchise is in place and strong, and absent our troubled portfolio, our core business earned $1.5 billion in 1991." That's the same as saying if we didn't lose our shirt, we would have had a good year. Surprisingly, no one, not even the usual stockholder meeting gadflies who were in attendance, said a word.

Reed then went on to discuss the first-quarter earnings. They were better than in the fourth quarter of 1991, but that's about all. And they were not even in the same ballpark as the quarterly earnings from a year ago (which have been restated to reflect accounting changes over the handling of the investment of venture capital subsidiaries).

The first quarter of 1992 showed little letup in the problems with Citicorp's commercial and real estate loan portfolio. In fact, the bank has decided to report its North American Commercial Real Estate as a separate category. This way, it won't drag down other commercial lending that (one hopes) may improve. In the first quarter of 1992, this new category showed a loss of $362 million; this compares with a loss of $86 million in the year-earlier period. For the first half of 1992, North American Commercial Real Estate write-offs totaled $718 million; in the similar period in 1991, the total was $176 million. Reported separately or not, nearly three-quarters of a billion dollars is quite a drag on earnings.

The Canadian Caper

There is no better example of the deteriorating real estate loan portfolio held by Citicorp than the financial woes of Olympia & York (O&Y), the Toronto-based real estate conglomerate. The firm, owned by the Reichmann family, which usually plays things close to the vest, had become the largest real estate developer in the world, with its projects altering the skylines of many cities in the United States and abroad.

Because of the way the firm was operated, there was little or no warning of the problems facing the company or how serious they turned out to be. Saddled with some $18 billion in debt, O&Y chief executive Paul Reichmann tried for months to restructure about $12 billion of that amount. Negotiations with its army of lenders worldwide fell short of what was needed, and Olympia & York filed for bankruptcy.

Citicorp is one of about 100 banks holding Olympia & York debt. Along with the four largest Canadian banks, Citi has one of the more substantial exposures, with nearly $500 million in outstanding loans. It wrote off $100 million during the first quarter of 1992, but that still leaves $380 million on the books—and only $100 million of that total is classified as performing. The outlook for this account is hardly bright, and has already led to some heads rolling at Citicorp (see Chapter 11).

Yet another example of Citicorp's real estate woes is the $120 million loss the bank sustained when it put the British property company, Randsworth Acquisition, Ltd., in receivership following the collapse of a restructuring agreement with JMB Realty of Chicago. Citi had an exposure of $335 million in Randsworth. The bank may have already written down its exposure, and John Reed says its London real estate portfolio has been cleaned up.

Holding On for Dear Life

The problem is that Citicorp is the largest lender in the United States to the real estate market. As Dianne Glossman, banking analyst at Salomon Brothers, observed, "We expect there will be more charges for real estate in the future."

There are indications that Citicorp is taking a long-term approach to its horrible real estate portfolio and holding the assets acquired and not selling them until the market improves. This is essentially the same kind of approach the bank took with its LDC loans to Latin America. Holding the real estate (there's that OREO again) can be costly, but there really is little choice. After all, how much of a write-off can one bank take, even a very large bank?

As the real estate market improves, of course, you will see Citicorp jumping in and trying to unload some of its properties. You can be sure this is what it is hoping to do with the Plaza Hotel. This is what the bank did in March 1992 when it sold an office complex in Indianapolis for $115 million. Citi was the lender to the developer of the complex, called Bank One Center. It was the lead bank (with three others) in a $181 million mortgage. The developer, Galbreath Company of Columbus, paid off $26 million, but when nothing more was forthcoming, Citicorp foreclosed on the property. Actually, the buyer of the property, Zell/Merrill Lynch Real Estate Opportunity Partners, an investment fund, put up only about 25 percent in cash; Citi took a mortgage on the balance.

While there are a few bright spots in Citicorp's commercial loan portfolio, the picture is not bright. And the real estate portfolio is even worse. As John Reed described it to a meeting of security analysts, "The real estate portfolio has turned out to be an immense problem."

If nothing else, Reed has become a master of understatement.

3

A Matter
of Management

If anything has set Citicorp apart from the pack of major U.S. banks, it has been its smart, assured, aggressive—and usually very effective—management. The banking company has been known, not only for its strong and able leadership at the top, but for the depth of its managerial resources throughout almost every segment of its far-flung operations—and rightly so. Citicorp's executive power, combined with a little bit of luck, has brought the bank through both good and bad years for the last century.

That very fact, however, leads to this obvious question: If management has been so terrific, why is Citicorp in the shape it's in?

The appropriate answer is that maybe management hasn't always been as good as it has often been perceived. And perhaps more to the point, there may be significant deficiencies in the management that is in place today.

As in almost every instance where a corporation has gotten into difficulties, there are extenuating circumstances; that certainly is true at Citicorp. One can look at the bank's broad array of problems and blame the economy, which has caused many of its loans to sour and some business volume to diminish. One can point to decisions made and actions taken a number of years ago that only recently have resulted in problems. One can also point to the changing competitive situation in the financial industry, both here and abroad. And one can underscore how rapidly and dramatically the business of banking has changed as technological advances have revolutionized bank operations.

These and other factors have surely impacted on Citicorp—as they have on almost any other financial institution you can name. The bottom line is how a bank's management has coped with such factors and how that management is dealing with them today. In Citicorp's case, after weighing in all the variables, one can reach only one conclusion: The present management of the company—at least, as demonstrated up to now—simply has not measured up to the challenges confronting the banking company in the 1990s.

1984 and 1985

It was in the summer of 1984 that Walter Wriston stepped down after 38 years with the organization, from 1967 to 1970 as president and from 1970 to 1984 as chairman and chief executive officer. He had a profound effect on Citicorp and, for that matter, the banking industry in this country and around the world. (See Chapter 6 and Part 3 for more on Wriston and the Wriston years.) However, Wriston had reached the bank's retirement age, and it was time for a new management team to take command.

Walter Wriston's replacement was selected from three officers who had solid, though each quite different, credentials with the organization:

- Hans Angermueller, Vice Chairman, Legal and External Affairs (Citiese for regulatory matters). At age 59, he was the oldest of the three finalists but the youngest in terms of service with the organization.
- John Reed, Vice Chairman, Individual Bank Operations. At 45, he was the youngest of the trio, and he had been with Citi since 1965. He was also the resident expert on technology and its application to banking.
- Thomas Theobald, Vice Chairman, Institutional Banking. With Citi since 1960, 47-year-old Theobald had the broadest and most extensive banking experience of the three contenders.

The contest really was between the two younger men; if Angermueller had been given the nod, he could only have been considered a caretaker chief until someone else was ready to take over. As it worked out, John Reed was deemed ready and able and the best person available to do the job. It was also generally understood, at least among those in the know in the bank, that he was Walter Wriston's favorite, and that didn't hurt one bit. The year "1984" had become famous in literature as a time in which futuristic, faceless government would be in power. All it meant at Citicorp was that new leadership was in place and that leadership seemed bent on continuing, in large measure, the direction and pace set by Wriston.

Staying the Course for a While

After John Reed was elected chairman and chief executive officer in the summer of 1984, he actively tried to maintain, and improve upon, the cordial and generally friendly relations he had always had with his former management rivals at Citicorp. He even went so far as to physically relocate Citicorp's executive suite, with offices arranged so as to foster a collegial atmosphere among the senior management team. This move seemed to be one way to demonstrate a break with the somewhat acerbic leadership of his predecessor without upsetting things too much. Besides, such a concept has had considerable success at several other banks, most notably J. P. Morgan.

Hans Angermueller, of course, was not a major priority of Reed's, since he seemed to be more lawyer than banker and was getting close to retirement age. That situation would take care of itself in relatively short order.

Tom Theobald was another matter. In fact, many people, both inside and out of the bank, had considered Theobald to have been the most apt choice to replace Wriston, regardless of the close relationship Reed enjoyed with the retiring chairman. Theobald had built a strong constituency at the bank; he was extremely able (his institutional bank was extremely profitable); and Reed well understood he could be invaluable in smoothing the transition from the old regime to the new.

Fine-Tuning the Lineup

During the next year or so, Reed made some attempts to put his stamp on Citicorp management, although the changes were hardly extensive; some say they were half-hearted, at best. Perhaps he was following that old saying, "If it ain't broke, don't fix it." The performance of Citicorp during the early 1980s seemed to indicate that there was, indeed, nothing broken. However, in September 1985 Reed did announce some changes.

There were three core businesses of the bank, then named the individual, institutional, and investment banks. The most extensive changes were made in the investment bank, where Theobald took charge at the behest of Reed. The assignment was sweetened with a number of additional services being placed under the investment bank's umbrella of responsibilities, such as money-market activities and foreign-exchange trading.

That move seemingly took care of one possible trouble spot. It had been rumored that Theobald might leave, but instead he took on a more significant position within the Citicorp organization.

Addressing this situation regarding his former rival, Reed said in an interview, "I think we've worked together spectacularly well. He's signed up to do this job. It reflects a deep-seated commitment on his part. He's on the cutting edge of a lot of what we're doing."

Richard (Rick) Braddock, who had been in charge of the individual bank's domestic business under Reed, was promoted to sector executive responsible for the individual bank. In effect, he succeeded Reed in that position.

Lawrence Small was appointed a sector executive in charge of the institutional bank, replacing Theobald. Previously, Small had been in charge of the North American Banking Group of the institutional bank and was credited with turning around that part of the division.

The new top leadership team at Citicorp, then, was composed of Reed, Theobald, Braddock, and Small. Braddock and Small were the same age (44) when the changes were made. Of the group, Theobald was the oldest and had been with the bank the longest. As it turned out, he was the first to leave.

There were three others who, as management directors, were considered part of the top team although, in fact, they weren't quite as equal to Reed and his three sector executives. These officers were Angermueller; senior corporate officer Paul J. Collins, who was chief planning officer, and was appointed to the new position of senior corporate officer for North America; and James D. Farley, a respected workhorse who was then a vice chairman responsible for, among other things, international debt restructurings. The new result of the management realignment (if that is the right word), according to a press account at the time, was that the changes were "nonrevolutionary."

It soon became apparent that the most equal member of the seven-man team of "equals" was Braddock. It should be remembered that he had been placed in charge of Reed's favorite business segment, the individual bank. Somewhat less equal—it's difficult to say how much less equal—was Larry Small, who had replaced Theobald at the institutional bank.

The Leadership Exodus
Theobald's Indecision on Leaving: First No, Then Yes

Although Theobald will not say so, it is more than likely he was deeply disappointed with the decision not to name him as Wriston's successor. Still, for a while, he thought things might work out satisfactorily; more than that, he was willing to see how things played out.

During the summer of 1984, right after Reed had been named the new chairman but before the changeover was official in August, Theobald was on the top of the short list prepared by the federal regulators who were trying to salvage Continental Illinois Bank in Chicago and in need of a new chief executive. At the time, Continental was reeling from the Penn Square scandal, compounded by generally bad management, and most assuredly it would have collapsed without massive federal intervention. A strong banker was needed to oversee what the regulators hoped would be the rebuilding of what once was America's fifth largest, and perhaps most respected, commercial bank.

FDIC officials felt out Theobald about the Continental job. He was an appropriate choice, considering the long history of Continental in the corporate banking business and Theobald's record of accomplishment at Citicorp in this same area. However, he unhesitatingly brushed off the overture, saying he would not take the position under any circumstances.

After others turned down the position—which is not surprising, considering the challenges that a new chief executive would face—the FDIC decided to have a comanagement team run Continental: John Swearingen, who had recently retired as chairman of Standard Oil of Indiana; and William Ogden, who had left Chase Manhattan the year before as vice chairman and chief financial officer. This arrangement would, it was felt, give Continental a combination of executive firepower and banking savvy. Though hardly an ideal arrangement, the team was able to hold the organization together. Both men naturally wanted to be the main boss, and Swearingen seemed to have the upper hand.

After a couple of years of correct but not the most cordial relations between the two men, Ogden left Continental. During the spring of 1987, Swearingen heard stories that Theobald had finally become dissatisfied at Citicorp. Well, it was true that his authority had been usurped, plus there was the obvious fact that with Reed in command, there was no place for Theobald to move. Would Theobald be more receptive this time around?

John Swearingen first contacted Tom Theobald during the spring of 1987. He had been with Continental longer than he had hoped, and he realized there was a need for a younger man who would be in place for the long haul. After satisfying Theobald's requirements, Swearingen offered him the position of chairman and chief executive officer. Theobald accepted the offer, leaving Citicorp and joining Continental in August 1987.

By and large, Tom Theobald has performed well at Continental, in what has to have been one of the toughest and more challenging jobs in American banking in recent years. Continental has come back a considerable distance from its low point in the mid-1980s, but it still has a long way to go. It is much smaller than what it used to be (and smaller than the assets managed by Theobald at Citicorp). But its recent performance in some respects puts it ahead of Citicorp, as an *American Banker* survey of money-center banks comparing first-quarter 1992 results with 1991 full-year results shows:

Return on Average Assets (ROA)

Rank			ROA	
1Qtr '92	1991		1Qtr '92	1991
2	8	Continental	1.02	−0.31
8	7	Citicorp	7.11	−7.78

Return on Average Equity (ROE)

Rank			ROE	
1Qtr '92	1991		1Qtr '92	1991
3	8	Continental	15.771	−9.22
8	7	Citicorp	7.11	−7.78

Continental also had a ration of performing assets below many of the other money-center banks, including Chemical and Chase.

The First to Go

Actually, the leadership exodus from Citicorp had begun earlier during Reed's tenure. One of the first and more prominent of those who left Citicorp was Richard M. Kovacevich, a senior vice president who was in charge of Citicorp's overseas consumer business and a member of the policy committee when he left in 1985. At age 40, Kovacevich saw little chance of breaking into the inner circle; he also was probably impatient to use his broad experience at Citicorp. Moreover, he was not enamored with all of Citi's philosophy.

"When I first went to Citibank," he said, "I was told the bank's market share was 33 percent, which is pretty good. But it turned out the market share was only about 4 percent. That was because the competition was considered to be only the other money center commercial banks. Other banks and thrifts were not included. [I believe] it is absolutely crucial that one understands who one is competing with."

He was recruited as vice chairman and head of the banking group at Norwest Corporation in Minneapolis during the spring of 1986. Norwest was in the process of restructuring itself after some rough times during the early 1980s. The move brought Kovacevich to a banking institution where he was able, as he puts it to "be in a leadership position against the total marketplace." This marketplace, he pointedly notes, includes such firms as Sears Roebuck, brokers, insurance companies, "and everyone else in the business of helping customers invest their funds." And this group definitely includes his former employer, Citicorp.

Kovacevich is now president of Norwest and heir apparent to the position of chairman and chief executive officer of the company. During the past couple of years, Norwest has been doing very well indeed. *Business Week* places it second to Banc One among midwest banks in the market value of its stock (and not that far behind Citicorp, although Norwest's assets are only one-fifth of the bigger bank's). Norwest's earnings in 1991 were well ahead of 1990, and the outlook for the current year is considered very good to excellent by most analysts.

Managers Coming and Going

A look at the end of this chapter at the list of senior Citicorp officers shows that only Kovacevich and one other (Frederick Roesch, who returned to the Citi fold in 1991) left in 1985. In 1987, several more left, including Tom Theobald. Two years later, in 1989, Hans Angermueller took early retirement at age 62.

It was in 1991, however, that three senior members of the leadership team left. Jim Farley reached retirement age. The two others, however, had been close associates of John Reed—Michael Callen and Lawrence Small.

It is also worth noting that in 1990 and 1991, the list of senior managers was greatly expanded. This happened at the same time that the bank instituted its "Five-Point Plan" to restore Citicorp's momentum. Point number two, it might be noted, is "Manage differently to reduce the cost base and improve the revenue/expense relationship." While there have been significant cost reductions since the beginning of 1991, and although the number of employees has decreased substantially, the bank has had difficulty trying to be lean and mean when the ranks of top management are steadily increasing. As an aside, there are only 6 women out of a total of approximately 93 senior management personnel shown in the 1991 annual report, although Citi officials say that the percentage of women in senior management positions is now "slightly more than 10 percent." (The company defines senior management as senior decision-making positions.) Does the National Organization of Women know about this?

The 1992 Top Management Team

The top management team has changed drastically in the eight years John Reed has been chief executive. The most recent change, and certainly the most dramatic, was the unexpected resignation of Richard Braddock, who had been elected Citicorp and Citibank president in 1989 and was Reed's second-in-command. There was considerable speculation as to the reason for the resignation. The speculation was hardly tempered by the statement issued by the bank that "Mr. Braddock chose to resign after concluding that his best contribution to the recovery of Citicorp's momentum has been realized [he had been given the responsibility for cutting costs] and, accordingly, he wants to pursue new career opportunities."

As a result of this latest departure, Reed's senior management team consists of three vice chairmen—Paul J. Collins, William S. Rhodes, and H. Onno Ruding (worldwide corporate banking activities). The fifth member is senior executive vice president Pei-yuan Chia (consumer banking worldwide).

There are two things that stand out in looking at the present team of managers under Reed. First, there is a decidedly international flavor to the team. This is logical because of the continued strong international presence of Citicorp. It might also signify the future direction of the organization. Interestingly, Ruding and Chia are the newest members, and Ruding has been with Citicorp for less than two years.

Also, and perhaps less apparent, is the fact that finally, after eight years, Reed has a top management team in place that can be said to be really his own. A chief executive must have his or her own team if that person has any hope of being effective as the leader of his corporation. But should it take eight years to accomplish this? And while each person on the team is recognized as being able and of high quality, does the team have the imagination and the aggressiveness needed to move Citicorp through the choppy financial waters ahead and into the twenty-first century?

Management Isn't Getting It Done

The problems at Citicorp that have surfaced during the 1980s and 1990s are due in large measure to a failure of management.

The real estate portfolio, which promises to continue to be a drag on earnings for an extended period of time—and a roadblock to growth at a time when other banks are fast closing in on Citicorp—has hardly been managed with style. Lawrence Small and Michael Callen, who both had major responsibilities in this area, somewhat unceremoniously left the organization. But have their replacements been any improvement?

For that matter, as already noted, the top management team, although all capable individuals, do not overwhelm with their dynamism. Do they have the kind of spirit and creativity Citicorp needs during these difficult times?

Yet spirit and creativity, together with solid ability, are what is needed in banking, circa 1992. And if any banking company in the United States is in need of these ingredients, it is Citicorp.

It can be said that John Reed has been slow to act. The high promise shown early in his stewardship (the write-offs of the Latin American debt) has not been followed by much action, and certainly not decisive action.

There are signs of late that he is actually taking command, that he is finally doing some of the things that could have been done, and should have been done, years ago. That raises a logical question: Is the leadership of the organization doing what must be done to move Citicorp forward? Or is it a matter of too little, too late?

As we shall see in later chapters, the answer to that last question might be in the affirmative.

Citicorp and Citibank Directors Under Reed (and the Length of Their Tenure)

	1984	1985	1986	1987	1988	1989	1990	1991
Hans H. Angermueller+^ Vice chairman, Citicorp and Citibank	x	x	x	x	x			
Richard E. Braddock+^ Sector executive, Citicorp and Citibank		x	x	x	x	x	x	x
Michael A. Callen+^ Sector executive, Citicorp and Citibank		x	x	x	x	x	x	
D. Wayne Calloway+ Chairman and CEO, PepsiCo					x	x	x	x
Colby H. Chandler+^ Chairman and CEO, Eastman Kodak	x	x	x	x	x	x	x	x
Paul J. Collins+^ Senior corporate officer, Citicorp and Citibank		x	x	x	x	x	x	x
Kenneth T. Derr+ Vice chairman, Chevron				x	x	x	x	x
John M. Deutch+ Provost, M.I.T.				x	x	x	x	x
James H. Evans+^ Chairman, Union Pacific	x	x	x	x	x			
James D. Farley+^ Vice chairman, Citicorp and Citibank	x	x	x	x	x	x	x	
Lawrence E. Fouraker+^ Professor emeritus, Harvard Grad. Bus. School	x	x	x	x	x	x	x	x
Arthur Furer+ Chairman, Bank Leu, Ltd.	x	x	x					
Clayton C. Garvin, Jr.+^ Chairman and CEO, Exxon	x	x	x	x	x	x	x	x

Citicorp and Citibank Directors Under Reed (and the Length of Their Tenure) (*Continued*)

	1984	1985	1986	1987	1988	1989	1990	1991
J. Peter Grace+^ Chairman and CEO, W.R. Grace	x							
Harry J. Gray+^ Chairman and CEO, United Technologies	x	x	x	x				
John W. Hanley+^ Former chairman, Monsanto	x	x	x	x	x	x	x	x
John P. Harbin+^ Former chairman, Halliburton	x	x						
H. J. Haynes+^ Senior counselor, Bechtel Group	x	x	x	x	x	x	x	x
Amory Houghton, Jr.+^ Chairman, Exec. Comm., Corning Glass	x	x	x					
Paul Kolterjahn^ Senior VP–secretary, Citicorp and Citibank	x							
Juanita M. Kreps+ Former U.S. Sec'y of Commerce	x	x	x	x	x			
C. Peter McColough+^ Chairman, Xerox	x	x	x	x	x	x	x	x
Roger Milliken+^ Chairman and CEO, Milliken & Co.	x	x	x					
Charles M. Pigott+^ President, PACCAR	x	x	x	x	x			
John S. Reed+^ Chairman, Citicorp and Citibank	x	x	x	x	x	x	x	x
William R. Rhodes+^ Vice chairman, Citicorp and Citibank								x

Citicorp and Citibank Directors Under Reed (and the Length of Their Tenure) (*Continued*)

	1984	1985	1986	1987	1988	1989	1990	1991
Rozanne L. Ridgway+ President, Atlantic Council							x	x
H. Onno Ruding+ Chairman, Netherlands Christian Federation Employers							x	x
Donald V. Seibert+^ Former chairman, J.C. Penney	x	x	x	x	x	x	x	x
Frank Shrontz+ President and CEO, Boeing			x	x	x	x	x	x
Irving S. Shapiro+ Former chairman, E.I. Du Pont	x							
Mario Henrique Simonsen+ Vice chairman, Brazilian Inst. of Econ.	x	x	x	x	x	x	x	x
Lawrence M. Small+^ Sector executive, Citicorp and Citibank		x	x	x	x	x	x	
Darwin E. Smith+^ Chairman and CEO, Kimberly-Clark	x	x	x					
Roger B. Smith+ Chairman and CEO, General Motors				x	x	x	x	x
Thomas C. Theobald+^ Vice chairman, Citicorp and Citibank	x	x	x					
Franklin A. Thomas+^ Vice chairman, The Ford Foundation	x	x	x	x	x	x	x	x
Edgar S. Woolard, Jr.+ President and CEO, E.I. Du Pont				x	x	x	x	x

+Director of Citicorp
^ Director of Citibank
SOURCE: Citicorp Annual Reports 1984–1991

Citicorp Senior Management Under Reed (and the Length of Their Tenure)

	1984	1985	1986	1987	1988	1989	1990	1991
Hans H. Angermueller	x	x	x	x	x			
James L. Bailey						x	x	x
Robert D. Bailey		x	x	x	x	x		
Richard S. Braddock	x	x	x	x	x	x	x	x
Ernst W. Brutsche						x	x	x
Michael A. Callen	x	x	x	x	x	x	x	
Pei-yuan Chia			x	x	x	x	x	x
Paul J. Collins	x	x	x	x	x	x	x	x
Colin Crook						x		
George L. Davis				x	x	x		
James D. Farley	x	x	x	x	x	x	x	
Pamela P. Flaherty			x	x	x		x	x
David E. Gibson			x	x	x	x	x	x
Paul F. Glaser						x		
Lawrence R. Glenn	x	x	x	x	x	x	x	x
Dennis O. Green						x	x	x
Guenther E. Greiner			x	x	x	x	x	x
George E. Hagerman, Jr.	x	x	x	x				
William J. Heron, Jr.			x	x	x	x	x	
Edwin P. Hoffman	x	x	x					
Donald S. Howard	x	x	x					
Anthony C. Howkins	x	x						
Richard L. Huber	x	x	x					
Daniel T. Jacobsen	x	x	x	x	x			
Thomas E. Jones	x	x	x	x	x	x	x	x
Michael B. Kelland						x	x	
Mark E. Kessenich	x	x						
Paul Kolterjahn	x	x	x					
Richard M. Kovacevich	x							
Phillip B. Lassiter				x	x	x	x	
Richard J. Lehmann	x	x	x					
Gerald M. Lieberman						x	x	x
Charles E. Long	x	x	x	x	x	x	x	x
Alan S. MacDonald			x	x	x	x	x	x
Anthony G. Mantzavinos	x	x	x	x	x			
Robert H. Martinsen				x	x	x	x	x
Victor Menezes			x	x	x	x	x	x
Sandra W. Meyer						x	x	x
Glen R. Moreno	x	x	x					
Patrick J. Mulhern	x	x	x	x	x			
Nancy S. Newcomb				x	x	x	x	x
William R. Rhodes	x	x	x	x	x	x	x	x
Ira S. Rimerman		x	x	x	x	x	x	x
John J. Roche					x	x	x	x
Frederick A. Roesch	x							x
Peter H. Schuring	x	x	x	x	x	x		
Lawrence M. Small	x	x	x	x	x	x	x	

Citicorp Senior Management Under Reed (and the Length of Their Tenure) (*Continued*)

	1984	1985	1986	1987	1988	1989	1990	1991
Sheridan L. Steinberg					x	x	x	x
Thomas C. Theobald	x	x	x					
Roger W. Trupin						x	x	x
David S. Van Pelt	x	x	x	x	x	x	x	x
Alan J. Weber					x	x	x	x
Lawrence D. Weiss						x	x	
Michael T. Welch						x	x	x

SOURCE: Citicorp Annual Reports 1984–1991

Senior Officers Added by Reed in 1990 and 1991

During 1990 and 1991, the senior officer group was greatly expanded. During those years, the following people were added:

	1990	1991
Dominick J. Agostino	x	
William B. Aimetti		x
Margaret G. Alton	x	
Roberta J. Arena		x
Shaukat Aziz	x	
Steven K. Baker	x	
Rodney F. Ballek	x	
Gerard P. Beitel	x	
Antonio M. Boralli	x	
Robert D. Botjer		x
David A. Brooks	x	
David J. Browning		x
Barry C. Burkholder	x	
Peter R. Burnim	x	
Martha L. Byorum	x	
Mary A. Cirillo	x	
Thomas J. Cirillo		x
Stewart B. Clifford	x	
William T. Comfort		x
A. Ewan Copeland		x
Ian D. Cormack	x	
J. Eric Daniels	x	
Roger A. Davis	x	
Arthur M. deGraffried		x
Cris Deuters	x	
Elvaristo T. Do Amaral		x
Roberto V. Do Valle		x
Bert J. Einloth	x	
Joachim Faber		x
William H. Friesell	x	
Peter M. Gallant		x
Ronald E. Geesey		x
Steven L. Gerard	x	
Jeffrey R. Grandy	x	
Jack D. Guenther		x
H. Richard Handley	x	
Hari N. Hariharan	x	
Balentin E. Hernandez	x	
David R. Hexter	x	
A. Lincoln Hoffman III	x	
Edward A. Holmes		x
Robert D. Horner	x	
Amador Huertas		x
Gabriel Jaramillo		x
Claude Jouven		x

Senior Officers Added by Reed in 1990 and 1991 *(Continued)*

During 1990 and 1991, the senior officer group was greatly expanded. During those years, the following people were added:

	1990	1991
Timothy M. Kelley		x
Michael J. Kirkwood	x	
Kenneth K. Knapp		x
Dimitri P. Krontiras		x
Tatsuo Kubota	x	
Robert N. Laughlin		x
David W. C. Leong	x	
Antony K.C. Leung	x	
Carl E. Levinson	x	
Clifford F. Lewis	x	
Robert A. McCormick	x	
Richard G. McCrossen	x	
John McFarlane		x
G. Patrick McGunagle	x	
Philip M. Markert	x	
Dennis R. Martin	x	
G. Edward Montero	x	
John L. Newbold III	x	
Aldo D. Palmeri		x
Nanoo G. Pamnani	x	
Steve H. Price	x	
Raymond J. Quinlan	x	
Robert H. Rosseau	x	
Francis A. Rozario	x	
Junaid M. Rubbani	x	
H. Onno Ruding		x
Hubertas Rukavina		x
Gerald R. Saltzgaber	x	
Carlos A. Salvatori	x	
Julian Simmonds		x
Todd J. Slotkin	x	
Loren E. Smith	x	
Richard J. Srednicki	x	
Albert F. Stevenson		x
James R. Stojak	x	
Rana S. Talwar	x	
G. Truett Tate	x	
Robert E. Terkhorn	x	
Bruce M. Weber	x	
Peter R. Wilde	x	
Donald A. Winkler	x	
Masamoto Yashiro	x	
Ronald X. Zettel	x	

SOURCE: Citicorp Annual Reports 1984–1991

PART 2

On Becoming Citicorp

We are on our way to bigger things. The National City Bank's future is brighter, I believe, than it has ever been. We have been going through a period of readjustment and a time of rebuilding. We are getting ready now to go ahead full speed.

Speech to Employees, 1922

Citicorp did not become a world-class financial organization overnight; if not for the almost offhand intervention of John Jacob Astor, it might not have celebrated its silver anniversary, let alone a 170th birthday in 1992.

In fact, the financial institution we know as Citicorp did not even come close to a top-rank bank until just before the advent of the twentieth century, and perhaps more precisely, after World War II. The organization experienced a long nurturing process. During that process there were plenty of mistakes made, countless examples of greed, varied cases of political intrigue, and serious problems nearly every inch of the way. And if that weren't enough, the troubles began even before the bank opened its doors for business.

The Citicorp saga is that of a particularly American institution, encompassing all sorts of pluses and minuses that may be associated with that designation. In fact, it is difficult to imagine a Citicorp happening anywhere else but in the United States.

The success of any organization, certainly the degree of success it may achieve over the years, is dependent to a great extent on its leadership. It is its leadership that shapes the organization, that gives it direction, that moves it along, that provides the basis for its character and its culture and yes, that can also be the cause of its problems. This has most assuredly been true at Citicorp. There have been a number of exceptional people in charge of the bank, but Citicorp almost died before the first of them appeared on the scene.

Over the years, some of the leaders of what is now Citicorp have accomplished a great deal for the bank. They have demonstrated the ability to play the game as they found it. They have been able, when necessary (and on occasion at other times), to speak for the banking industry. They have helped to change, sometimes dramatically, the laws and regulations by which the industry has been governed—whether or not the changes have been ultimately advantageous for the industry. They have been innovators, developing new products and concepts, expanding the parameters of banking and finance. They have been rugged individualists and leaders of the corporate way of life. At the same time, it must be said that there have been those in positions of leadership who have shown what seemed to be little concern for some of the rules. And there have been times when they have failed miserably in achieving their objectives. But maybe it takes all that to be a great organization, a great bank. Clearly, Citicorp fits that bill.

These leaders are the people who have brought Citicorp through a period lasting 170 years, a longevity not many business organizations have experienced. But now, serious questions are being raised about this once-dynamic organization.

Citicorp is many things to many people, depending mostly on what dealings they have with the organization. For those without an intimate relationship with Citicorp, the image of the organization may not be all that great. At times, there were indications that the company (or, at least, its management) really didn't give a damn about the impression created by its actions. And the company's image may have changed from the time this book was written until now, when you are reading it.

To get a truly accurate picture of any institution as it exists today (and some clues as to why it is in the shape it's in and even what its prospects are for tomorrow), it is necessary to look at that institution's beginnings and its development over the years. With Citicorp, then, it seems most appropriate to begin at the beginning.

4
The First Hundred Years

Of course, Citicorp wasn't always Citicorp, in fact or in name. The company began its existence in 1812 as the City Bank of New York. That name was changed to The National City Bank of New York in 1865 when the company gave up its state charter and joined the national banking system, which had come into existence two years before. There were no further changes until 1955, when the bank merged with The First National Bank of the City of New York, a relatively small bank at the time but one with a blue-blood pedigree and a host of blue-chip customers; the resulting organization was called First National City Bank. The "New York" part of the name was dropped in order to lessen the image of a banking company limited to New York City—or to New York State, for that matter.

A one-bank holding company was formed in 1968, and First National City Bank became the lead bank in what was originally called the First National City Corporation. In 1974, the holding company's name was then changed to Citicorp and, two years later in 1976, the lead bank's name was changed to Citibank N.A. (for "National Association").

And that is how the name of a small banking company that was established in 1812 in New York City evolved into Citibank and Citicorp; the evolution of the organization itself has been far more complex.

A Bank of, by, and for Merchants

If you think our financial institutions have problems today, the situation is nothing like the turmoil and confusion and intrigue that existed in the United States in the early 1800s. The young nation was just beginning to grow and prosper and feel its oats. England was resentful of how well its former colony was doing, and the talk of war swept the land. To make matters worse, the political scene was extremely raucous, hardnosed, and dirty—much more so in those early days than ever since.

The fledgling banking system was dominated by the Bank of the United States, established in 1791 at the urging of Alexander Hamilton, the country's first secretary of the treasury. The Bank of the United States was, to put it mildly, in a class by itself. It possessed the only federal banking charter; it was the depository for most of the government's funds; and the notes it issued were the only ones accepted as legal tender throughout the country. Within a few years, its branch banking system ranged from Boston to New Orleans, and the influence it wielded was even more widespread. Those facts alone were enough to cause it to have enemies and adversaries everywhere, including Washington, D.C.

When the Bank of the United States' charter came up for renewal in 1810, there were many who felt the bank had become too powerful and that it limited the opportunities for financial entrepreneurs. After a bitter fight between the Federalists and advocates for stronger states rights, the charter renewal lost by one vote in the Senate after Vice President George Clinton broke a tie in 1811. That vote had a long-reaching effect because it effectively established a precedent against nationwide banking while supporting the principle of the regulation of banking by the individual states.

The demise of the Bank of the United States also made the market for banking companies in New York City even more attractive than it had been previously, now that a large and powerful competitor was out of the way.

Almost immediately, a group of merchants petitioned the government of the state of New York to charter a new bank to be known as "City Bank." However, since the organizers were primarily supporters of President James Madison (and since the nephew of the Vice President, New York Governor Dewitt Clinton, was gearing up to run against Madison the following year), politics worked against the merchants, and the charter was not approved by the state legislature.

When the legislature reconvened the following January, the City Bank petition was reactivated. A fight soon began brewing because another group wanted a charter so it could take over part of the business of the defunct Bank of the United States. That group, incidentally, planned to use the name of Bank of America. This only goes to show that the more things change, the more they remain the same.

Into the fray jumped Samuel Osgood, a staunch Republican who saw the charter battle as an opportunity to unite his party. He and his faction worked out a deal with the Bank of America group, which withdrew its petition, and then both sides agreed to name six directors to the proposed City Bank board, which may have been the first bipartisan banking organization in the United States. The charter was approved and the new bank opened for business on June 16, 1812, with $2 million in capital and Samuel Osgood as president.

Two days later, the government of the United States declared war against Great Britain.

War and Other Conflicts

The new bank, which basically had been formed to serve the financial interests of its merchant-owners, soon found itself in the business of helping to finance a war. That war included, among other things, a blockade that brought much-needed overseas commerce to a virtual halt, so the conflict worked out to be advantageous to the bank. The leaders of City Bank did what they could to advance the cause of the United States. As a reward, the struggling bank was designated a depository of the federal government. Before the war ended, City Bank held about one-third of the government's funds deposited in New York City.

After two-and-one-half years, in early January 1815, the war ended. Although the country was finally at peace, there was little time for the merchant-owners of City Bank to relax. New competition came in the form of the second Bank of the United States, which was chartered by Congress that year. As soon as this latest national bank was organized, the federal government withdrew most of its funds from state-chartered institutions, including City Bank.

Another problem facing the young bank was the fact that it simply had not conducted itself very conservatively or prudently during the war years. Money had been lent mostly to directors and to their friends, with little regard for the quality of the loan or of the borrower. With the economy in poor shape after the fighting stopped, many of these loans became overdue. After struggling along for another decade, the bank was on the ropes. Finally, new ownership and management took command of City Bank in 1825.

For a while, the fortunes of the bank improved. One of the new directors, Isaac Wright, who imported textiles from Great Britain, served as City Bank's fifth president, from 1827 to 1832, and the financial needs of his business helped the bank to survive. Also, during this period the economy slowly recovered, first with the opening of the Erie Canal (in

1825) and then with the advent of the railroad in the 1830s. Helping things along was the fact that the port facilities in New York grew rapidly, bringing in even more business.

There was one drawback, however. The second Bank of the United States was headquartered in Philadelphia, as was the case with the first bank. Consequently, even with its leadership as a (growing) center of commerce, New York was still not the financial capital of the country.

In addition, competition from some of the other banks in New York City began to hurt. For example, Chemical Bank, which had been chartered in 1824, fought hard for City Bank's loans and deposits, much as it is doing today with its added clout due to the merger of Chemical and Manufacturers Hanover Trust Company. Still another problem was that City Bank's loans to its directors continued to be a drag on earnings. With its lowered capitalization (it had dropped from $2 million to $1.5 million) and decreasing assets, the bank was unable to compete for some of the federal government's business which would otherwise have been available to it.

Then, compounding the situation, the second Bank of the United States began to have political troubles, throwing the banking system of the country into more confusion than usual. Calling the bank too powerful and too corrupt, and little more than a tool of its president, Nicholas Biddle, President Andrew Jackson battled with the bank during his successful election campaign in 1832. He vetoed an extension of the bank's charter, which meant it would go out of business when its current charter expired in 1836. After it did close down, the Bank of England, which was having problems of its own, sharply increased the discount rate. This led to a recession in Great Britain and eventually to the panic of 1837 here in the United States. Specie (coin, as opposed to notes) began to be withdrawn from many banks, and the cotton market collapsed. When depositors rushed to New York City banks demanding specie, the banks had to suspend payments. City Bank, already in a weakened position, was in deep trouble.

First of the Strong Leaders

One of the problems of City Bank during its first quarter century was the lack of leadership to match the challenges of the time. The first president, Osgood, was no banker, nor were any of the others that followed.

As the panic of 1837 worsened, City Bank was faced with an even greater decline in the circulation of its notes and a greater withdrawal of deposits than was being experienced by the other banks in New York. City Bank was near collapse when John Jacob Astor, then the richest man in the country, chose to support the foundering bank. He did this, not only by pumping in money, but by installing his personal representative, Moses Taylor, as a director.

From the moment Taylor entered the City Bank picture, he was in charge (although a man named Thomas Bloodgood was president at the time and continued into the mid-1840s). In effect, he changed the bank from one established to help a group of merchants to a bank in business to assist one particular merchant—Moses Taylor.

John Jacob Astor himself had little to do with City Bank or its operations. Taylor, who was no slouch as a businessman himself, had become associated with Astor several years earlier, and the older man treated him as a son. Astor was available to assist his protégé when and if needed; most of the time, however, Moses Taylor did not need any help, from Astor or anyone else. Taylor had many and varied business interests, and City Bank served as an ideal treasury for those interests. In order to facilitate his financial requirements as they arose, Taylor made sure that his bank had high liquidity and practiced prudent solvency standards, a concept not always followed at the bank in later years.

Taylor finally became president of City Bank in 1856, continuing to run it much as he had for nearly 20 years but also acquiring controlling equity interest at the same time. He may not have been the ideal leader, and he certainly could not be called a banker, but he did keep the bank in business, moving it ahead through some stormy times—and mostly in those directions that served his own financial interests.

The National Banking Act, which became law in 1863, established a true national banking system for the first time. Even with the rigors of a Civil War, the law quickly created a prestigious new group of banks which opened up different areas of banking business. Taylor decided it would be advantageous for his bank to partake of some of that prestige and so he converted the bank's charter from state to national status. While making these moves, he also changed the bank's name to National City Bank.

When Moses Taylor died in 1882, his personal wealth amounted to more than $33 million—far greater than the assets of his bank. His son-in-law and business partner, Percy Pyne, was promptly named president and continued running the bank in the same Taylor tradition. During the Taylor and Pyne dynasty, the bank weathered three panics—in 1857, 1873, and 1884. In all three of those economic upheavals, the bank was able to increase its deposits, while competing New York banks, on average, lost. Actually, National City Bank grew in tandem with the fortunes of the Taylor family: The bank's assets went from $1.7 million in 1837 when Moses Taylor first became a director, to $22.2 million in 1891, when Percy Pyne was forced to resign after suffering a stroke.

The Bankers Arrive—Finally

At the end of the Taylor-Pyne years, National City had grown substantially, but it was still only two-thirds the size of Chemical Bank, which had become the largest commercial bank in New York City. National City was generally profitable, but mainly that was because expenses were kept low and it did not issue its own notes.

Another merchant, James Stillman, was elected to the presidency after Percy Pyne resigned. Supposedly Stillman was chosen because he was just about the only person available, and also because he seemed to be capable. These factors may have been accurate, since Moses Taylor had kept the bank quite small in order to keep expenses low. There were only two officers, the president and the cashier, so there weren't a whole lot of people to choose from in selecting a president. As things turned out, Stillman proved to be something not realized by the other directors—a banking whiz.

Perhaps the major difference between Taylor and Stillman was that the former was basically an industrialist and the latter was a financier. As such, Stillman emphasized and built upon his (and his bank's) relationships with customers. And these customers were some of the biggest names in American business during the latter part of the nineteenth century—Rockefeller, Harriman, Kuhn, McCormick. Their businesses used National City to hold their deposits, and the resulting growth was phenomenal. For example, Stillman was a close friend of William Rockefeller, the brother of John, who was the founder of Standard Oil. That company funneled so much of its funds through National City that some called it the "Standard Oil Bank." The friendship continued, William became a major investor in the bank, and two of Stillman's daughters married two of William Rockefeller's sons.

By 1905, City had assets of $308 million—over 25 percent more than the second largest bank in the country at the time (the National Bank of Commerce).

Because of his contacts and his interests, Stillman was able to broaden the business of the bank, moving it into investment banking, the financing of foreign trade, and correspondent banking. In so doing, he strengthened the institution. Not only did National City survive the panic of 1907, it actually became stronger.

The move into a leadership position in correspondent banking happened in 1897 when the Third National Bank failed. One of the principal owners, who was also counsel to National City, arranged a merger between the banks. The Comptroller of the Currency, who had been president of Third National, A. B. Hepburn, became a National City vice president and was placed in charge of the merger.

Within two years, Hepburn resigned to become president of Chase National Bank. But he was replaced by Frank A. Vanderlip, who had been recommended to Stillman by Lyman Gage, the secretary of the treasury. Vanderlip, who was Gage's assistant, was brought along rapidly by Stillman, who recognized that his new officer had the makings of a winner.

The correspondent balances generated after the merger with Third National, combined with the corporate balances that had been growing extensively since Stillman became president, allowed National City—and James Stillman—to become a major player in the investment banking business.

In addition to wanting to make National City a national bank in every sense of the word (and some of the names mentioned in preceding paragraphs indicate that the organization was at last playing in the big leagues), Stillman wanted it to be *the* major bank for the federal government. By 1897, it was the largest depository for government funds. It then was designated to receive the tax revenues of the government and distribute them to other depository banks. In many ways Stillman had, in fact, made his bank the nation's bank.

An Emphasis on Capital

One aspect of Stillman's tenure cannot be overlooked—his concern that the bank have a strong capital base. Although aggressive in many of his business dealings, he also was conservative. He felt that sufficient capital was essential to the bank's underwriting activities and to the building of stockholder equity. In a letter to shareholders requesting an increase in capital, dated April 30, 1902, Stillman wrote:

> In the opinion of the Board, the business of the Bank can be further developed and extended by increasing its capital and surplus. The capital of the Bank is still small compared with the volume of its business, especially so compared with that of financial institutions in foreign countries, where a much broader basis of capitalization is customary and is deemed essential to a safe and conservative banking business. With a capital of $25,000,000, a shareholders' liability for the same amount and a surplus of $15,000,000, this Bank will command a higher degree of confidence, with results which it is believed will be a cause of substantial satisfaction to the shareholders.

James Stillman knew the value of a strong capital base, and his efforts made National City the best capitalized bank in the country at the time, resulting in substantial increases in both assets and profits. More recently, somewhere along the line, however, this concern for and devotion to the capital base has gotten lost. Now, as has been already noted and will be underscored again in later chapters, the bank is not the bank it used to be, in terms of capital.

Vanderlip and Stillman

At the end of 1908, National City moved across the street, from 52 to 55 Wall Street. The move symbolized the changes that had taken place since the election of James Stillman to the presidency. The bank had outgrown its old headquarters and needed something larger and grander. The new building was actually an old building but in the grand tradition, the former U.S. Customs House.

A few weeks later, in early 1909, Frank Vanderlip was elected president. At the same time, Stillman moved up to the newly created title of chairman of the board.

The change turned out to be more substantial than just a change in titles. Despite all the bank's achievements, James Stillman had built the bank primarily on personal relationships. It had grown substantially over the years, with increasing numbers of officers and employees. But it was still essentially a one-man bank. However, at the time, in the early part of the twentieth century, major developments were occurring in American business, and this certainly affected the banking business. While personal relationships remained important (and undoubtedly always will), business was turning more to the professional manager and away from the individual owner. Business firms were becoming too large and too complex for one person to run it all. These managers were increasingly the ones who made financing decisions, and they could relate to bankers who were also managers in similar capacities at their institutions.

As a result, it was necessary to institutionalize the relations of the bank with its customers and investors in order to deal with the changes taking place. It soon became apparent that Frank Vanderlip was the ideal person for overseeing these far-reaching changes in the way banking was done. At the same time, Stillman remained the true power in the bank, although he readily and usually enthusiastically delegated his authority to Vanderlip. As Vanderlip grew into the job, Stillman spent less and less time at the bank, often spending months in Europe. The new man was, for all intents and purposes, running the bank.

Wrestling With Reform

Not only was there an obvious need to change the relationships between the bank and customers at National City, there was growing acceptance of the fact that there was a need for radical changes in the regulation of banking.

The industry in the 1900s simply was not the same as it was when the last major banking legislation had been enacted in 1863. The panic of 1907, especially, focused attention on the desirability of a central bank. J. Piermont Morgan, along with James Stillman and National City Bank, were instrumental in providing funds to other institutions to keep the financial system afloat. But a real central bank would be able to do a much better job, and it would allow private institutions such as National City to do other things to shore up the system in emergency situations.

Frank Vanderlip, as president of the largest bank in the country, with his experience at the Treasury Department, was a most appropriate participant in discussions regarding a possible central bank.

Senator Nelson Aldrich of Rhode Island was instrumental in enacting a law to provide emergency money to help stop the panic of 1907 (The Aldrich-Vreeland Act). Of course, that measure was designed to stop a panic, not prevent one from happening. So later Congress established a National Monetary Commission, with Aldrich in charge, to study the whole situation and develop a plan that would rid the economy of panics through the creation of a central banking system.

Because he knew little about the business of banking, Aldrich sought the help of financial experts. With his commission required to present the results of its studies and a plan of action in early 1911, Aldrich asked several people to meet secretly with him at Jekyll Island, near Brunswick, Georgia, where a number of millionaires kept summer homes. Their mission was to draft a plan for banking reform. Those he asked included Paul M. Warburg of Kuhn Loeb; Henry P. Davidson of J. P. Morgan; Benjamin Strong of Bankers Trust; Piatt Andrew, assistant secretary of the treasury; and Frank Vanderlip of National City Bank. Dressed as hunters, all but Strong made the long rail trip to south Georgia in the late fall of 1910.

The group came up with a plan for a national reserve association that would hold the reserves of the member banks, rediscount their commercial paper, and issue bank notes. It became known as the Aldrich plan, but it never got very far. Senator Aldrich became estranged from his fellow Republicans and never was good friends with the Democrats. In the long run, the fact that it was called the Aldrich plan probably hurt more than it helped.

After the Democrats took control of Congress and the White House in the 1912 elections, Senator Carter Glass proposed a plan that was similar to the Aldrich plan in many of its details, but control was to be placed in a politically appointed board. Vanderlip strongly opposed this aspect of the plan, wanting instead a central bank in which bankers would have control. While the Federal Reserve Act that was passed and signed into law in December 1913 was not the kind of central bank Vanderlip had wanted, it did allow National City to move more aggressively into a variety of private banking opportunities and, not incidentally, relinquish its quasi-public-policy role.

The Federal Reserve Act was designed to some extent to limit the powers of the big city banks. However, in reality, the new law actually helped increase business for those banks, including National City. In fact, in the four years from mid-1912 to mid-1916, the total number of corporate accounts at National City almost doubled. And in the three years from mid-1914 to mid-1917, the bank's commercial loans tripled, to $213 million. As Vanderlip said to Stillman, "It [The Federal Reserve Act] has made the City Bank far more a national bank than ever before."

During the early years of World War I, Vanderlip came to understand that if National City was to grow further on the international scene, the bank would have to do something to make customers want to choose his bank rather than the others clamoring for the same business. His solution was to open international branches, a move which was permitted to national banks under the new law. He did this, and because he acted so promptly, National City was in place in many overseas locations, particularly South America, before restrictive local laws were enacted. His bank was one-up on the competition.

Getting Around the Law. Frank Vanderlip was the first leader of the bank known today as Citicorp to try a means of expansion that later seemed to become a way of life for some administrations of the organization; he dearly wanted to form an affiliate that was not subject to the restrictions of the National Bank Act. Such an affiliate would allow National City to move into new territories, offering different kinds of services that would attract additional customers and help the bank to hold on to the customers it already had.

Actually, the owners of the bank had for some time put their money into trust companies and banks so that they could be involved in activities that National City, as a national bank, could not perform. Moses Taylor, for example, owned the Farmers' Loan and Trust Company. And James Stillman invested in a large number of banks and trust companies located both in New York City and throughout the country. But these were personal involvements; Vanderlip wanted to involve National City itself; he wanted to establish a corporate affiliate.

The concept had a willing ear at the Treasury Department. And some other banks had already established subsidiaries that made investments and transacted other business not within the scope of powers of a national bank.

Vanderlip made a proposal to the shareholders who then approved the formation of the National City Company, incorporated under the laws of the state of New York in July 1911. Not only was the affiliate immediately the largest in the country, it almost immediately became what we now call a bank holding company by acquiring the shares of other banks and trust companies owned by other shareholders and by such trustees as James Stillman. In some cases, the ownership was a small percentage; in others it was everything.

Without realizing it, Vanderlip, by dealing with antitrust issues, had touched upon a raw nerve. After loud rumblings in Congress about possible investigations of the "money trust," Vanderlip decided to back off and the affiliate divested itself of the domestic bank stocks in November 1911. The entire episode happened over the course of less than six months.

Things Change.   While new legislation was being enacted and the bank was moving into virgin territory, Frank Vanderlip was also looking ahead at his own personal situation. This was particularly so when Stillman came down with a serious illness in 1915. Vanderlip wanted to solidify his position at the bank and, indeed, in the financial world itself. He asked Stillman for a loan with which to buy more shares of National City stock, plus a block of stock in J. P. Morgan, which had been offered to him by J. P., Jr., himself.

When Stillman drastically scaled back what he would provide, Vanderlip indicated that he understood. But it hurt, regardless, and the episode subtlety changed the relations between the two men. And, a little later, when Vanderlip wanted to move from the presidency to a newly created position of vice chairman in order to free up time for handling his personal business, Stillman dragged his feet before finally agreeing, figuring that it might be impossible to find someone suitable for the job of president. This proved to be the case. So while there was a reorganization, nothing really changed—particularly between Stillman and Vanderlip.

Russian Roulette.   Nothing really happened, that is, until the Bolshevik revolution.

Vanderlip had long felt that Russia offered great opportunities for National City, and in 1916 he agreed to open a branch there. In fact, he felt the war would actually be beneficial to the bank, if he could establish branches all across Russia.

The first branch was opened in Petrograd in January 1917. Two months later, the revolution occurred, bringing in the Kerensky regime;

however, the bank remained open, and it even continued as a depository for the government. Then, on November 6, 1917, the Bolsheviks seized Petrograd and a month later the new government took over the banking system.

On the very day the Bolsheviks took power, so did James Stillman at National City in New York, taking over from Vanderlip who was then on leave in Washington as head of the War Savings Committee. Three months later, Stillman called Vanderlip back to New York for a meeting. While there are no details of what actually transpired at their meeting, it is hard to imagine that the topic of the bank branch lost due to the Russian situation was not included in the conversation.

It is also not known if Vanderlip had been asked to resign, because not long after the meeting, Stillman again became seriously ill and died a month later. Stillman's son, James A. Stillman, was immediately elected chairman. Vanderlip held on as president until well after the Armistice. However, the younger Stillman decided during the spring of 1919 to pull the rug out from under Vanderlip. As the former president declared in his book, *From Farm Boy to Financier* (D. Appleton Century, 1935), "I could have made a fight, but I cannot say too strongly that I welcomed the chance to get out."

Moving Forward.   In the space of three short years from 1914 to 1917, Frank Vanderlip worked an amazing transformation at National City Bank. Starting with an institution whose basic functions were to keep and invest the funds of correspondent banks in the United States and to provide financial services to corporations, he built upon this base, adding such new functions as international banking at a system of branches, worldwide banking at correspondent banks, and investment banking at an affiliate. National City gradually diversified, expanding its geographic influence internationally as this occurred. As has been observed, each new activity grew out of existing functions. What gave this development life, of course, was Vanderlip's strategic thinking, his dynamic vision of the bank.

In 1915, in a note to his mentor James Stillman, he wrote something that would prove to be amazingly prophetic: "We are really becoming a world bank in a very broad sense, and I am perfectly confident that the way is open to us to become the most powerful, the most serviceable, the most far-reaching world financial institution that there has ever been. The one limitation that I can see lies in the quality of management."

It always does.

Stillman and Mitchell and the Great Depression

James A. Stillman resigned as chairman and became president, succeeding Frank Vanderlip in June 1919. To put it charitably, James A. was not the banker his father was.

It wasn't long before troubles began brewing. The big problem was the Cuban sugar loan portfolio. Sugar prices collapsed and by the end of 1921, the bank's exposure to sugar amounted to 80 percent of the bank's total capital. Stillman didn't wait until then before resigning in May 1921. He left Charles E. Mitchell with the responsibility of coming up with a solution to the sugar loan crisis. It was felt that if anyone could resolve the situation, the man who in four years had made National City Company the largest distributor of securities in the United States could. Although one of the directors, Eric Swenson, was named chairman of the board, it was Mitchell who ran the show.

Taking Command

Charles Mitchell quickly took over the reins. By the end of 1921, National City's liquidity, which had been dangerously low, was increased substantially. Its borrowings from the Federal Reserve, which earlier in the year had amounted to three times the bank's required reserves, had all been repaid. The loan portfolio was cleaned. And marginal international branches were shut down.

The bank's sugar problems, however, remained. After investigating the situation and even making a special visit to Cuba to see what was happening, Mitchell decided to follow the recommendations of a study report and go heavily into the sugar business, betting that there would be a recovery of prices. Then, when sugar was healthy again, the bank's sugar assets could be unloaded at a profit. Prices did rise, but the recovery did not last, and the bank was stuck with a bunch of sugar mills. Some of those mills were not sold until 1945.

In other respects, after two years at the helm, Mitchell had accomplished a minor miracle. He also had solidified the place of the professional manager at Citicorp.

During the roaring twenties, National City became what could best be described as a financial department store under the leadership of Charles Mitchell. His flamboyant style brought a marketing energy to the bank, and the bank prospered. He added a local bank to Stillman's wholesale bank and to Vanderlip's international bank. Total deposits rose from $649 million in 1921 to $1.649 billion in 1929. For the first time, the bank concentrated on attracting the consumer or, as Mitchell called this customer, "the small but developing capitalist."

At the Brink

At the beginning of 1929, National City Bank was sitting pretty—or so it thought. The bank was strong and bigger—and more powerful—than ever. The National City Company, the affiliate that underwrote about a third of all bond issues in the United States, was known for its conservative investment advice, and its business boomed. To broaden and strengthen its trust business, a segment that had not expanded all that much, National City merged with Farmers' Loan and Trust in April 1929. The bank, Mitchell said, was ready for the future.

Then came that black Tuesday in October.

The next three years was a steep ride in one direction—down. Assets fell from $2.1 billion in 1929 to $1.6 billion in 1932. Loans dropped by 50 percent, deposits by 21 percent. Profits went from $23 million in 1929 to a loss of $12.6 million in 1932. The press depicted bankers such as Charles Mitchell as villains of the first degree.

In 1933, the Senate Banking Committee conducted hearings to fix the blame for the stock market crash and the resulting depression. The committee's chief counsel, Ferdinand Pecora, picked Charles Mitchell as the lead witness because of his position in the industry and because of what Pecora perceived as wrong actions taken by the bank. "National City was one of the very largest banks in the world," Pecora said later in the March 11, 1933, issue of *Literary Digest*, "and had only recently been surpassed in this country by Chase National. The prestige and reputation of these institutions were enormous. They stood, in the mind of the financially unsophisticated public, for safety, strength, prudence, and high-mindedness, and they were supposed to be captained by men of unimpeachable integrity, possessing almost mythical business genius and foresight."

Pecora was determined that was not the case, and he began his assault on the banking industry with Charles Mitchell. He brought out the fact that Mitchell had earned more than $1 million in 1929 but had paid no income tax that year because of a capital loss on the sale of National City stock to his wife.

Another part of the hearings discussed the call loan market—demand loans to brokers and securities dealers secured by stock and bonds—which had become the liquid asset most readily available after cash and bank deposits. Call loans were selling in record numbers in early 1929 when stock prices broke and call money rates jumped. National City moved in and propped up the market. In so doing, Mitchell stepped on some toes at the Federal Reserve, although most observers agreed that what the bank had done was precisely what had to be done.

Going over this controversy in testimony, the following exchange occurred:

> SENATOR BROOKHART: If you had let the call market collapse in March, that would have saved hundreds of thousands of dollars to people who invested later on, prevented them from buying, and the collapse would not have suffered such purchases to mean a loss. Is not that a fact?
>
> MR. MITCHELL: I do not believe that any man who has it within his power to stop a money panic is going to take the responsibility of seeing the money panic develop.
>
> SENATOR BROOKHART: That is what is wrong with our financial system; nobody is going to stop this speculation.

The senators generally agreed that the bankers had fueled the speculation, and the press agreed with the senators. Mr. Pecora later wrote in *Literary Digest* that the testimony of National City officers, and Mitchell's in particular, "an amazing recital of practices, to which the catastrophic collapse of the entire banking structure of the country seemed but the natural climax."

A governor of the Federal Reserve Board described Mitchell's testimony as embarrassing (which showed that the wounds from four years ago had not healed); he called for Mitchell's resignation. On February 26, 1933, Charles Mitchell did just that.

When *The New York Times* reported on March 6, 1933, that Mitchell's resignation had been accepted by National City Bank's board of directors, the caption under the picture of him that ran with the story read, "The Senators got their man."

5

From Postwar
to Moore

From the depths of the depression until the advent of George Moore in the 1950s, National City Bank struggled along under a mixed bag of leadership, and with performance figures that ran the gamut from so-so to acceptable.

The bank had its low point in 1934, when its losses were close to a record $60 million. James H. Perkins, who had been president of Farmers' Loan and Trust before and after being acquired by National City (and which had been renamed City Bank Farmers' Trust Company) had replaced Charles Mitchell as chairman and provided straight-arrow leadership with little imagination until the war years. This type of leadership was probably exactly what National City needed to recover from the depression's dark days.

It was in the Eisenhower years in the 1950s that the bank really began to move again, to some extent under the leadership of James Stillman Rockefeller, whose name perhaps provides all the background necessary to give one an idea of the man and his management style. His grandfathers were James Stillman and William Rockefeller; he could hardly escape becoming National City president. Ah, but could he have gotten the job if his name did not include those two former major players in the life of the bank?

Mergers and Failed Mergers

The Eisenhower era saw National City Bank merge with the First National Bank in 1955 to form the First National City Bank of New York. Fifty years previously, First National had been one of the premier banks in the country, the source of envy by the leaders of National City in those days. But it had fallen on hard times and was a fairly small bank by New York City standards at the time of the merger. However, its accounts still read like the Blue Book of American business. Without question, it was a natural marriage.

Then, in the latter part of the 1950s, First National City tried desperately to move into the affluent suburbs surrounding New York through the use of the new Bank Holding Company Act of 1956.

The first attempt, a merger with County Trust Company of Westchester County, met with opposition at the Federal Reserve; when the way was eventually smoothed out, County Trust was no longer available. The next candidate, the National Bank of Westchester, was much smaller, but it did provide an entry into the supposedly profitable suburbs.

As might be expected, First National City tried to show how it would bring competitive prosperity to the area with the merger. The memorandum to the Comptroller of the Currency read, in part:

> By careful, factual analysis, we have demonstrated that the proposed merger would make readily available to the residents and business firms of Westchester County the full range of services, the better quality of services, and the lower rates and charges of a large-scale, efficient New York City Bank. It would not alter the distribution of banking assets in Westchester. It would intensify competition, not only among the Westchester banks but among nonbank institutions as well. It would bring to the public in this part of the metropolis the benefits of the intense banking competition which exists in the city center. It would supply more healthy competition with the leading bank in the area. It would intensify competition not only in Westchester but throughout the entire New York Banking District. It would help one of the nation's major banks to continue to contribute to the economic progress of the nation.
>
> In view of these facts, which are documented in detail in this application, it is urged that the proposed merger be approved.

Comptroller James Saxon didn't buy it. But this presentation by Citicorp is illustrative of the mindset of the organization and its leadership after World War II; it prepared itself to make the most of the exciting banking opportunities beginning to open up worldwide after the war.

The memorandum illustrates a combination of near arrogance, a dash of patriotism, a recitation of the glories of competition, and a focus on several factors which presumably would appeal to the regulators. In this instance, that focus apparently had something to do with "intensity." Whatever, the proposal was not accepted.

Moore Is More

It was during the James Stillman Rockefeller years when he was National City president that George S. Moore played an increasingly important role in the management of the bank. Actually, it was Howard Sheperd, who was chairman in the 1950s after a short stint as president, who was most instrumental in the development of Moore.

George Moore came to First National City Bank from Farmers' Loan and Trust in 1929 when the two institutions merged. At the time, he was assistant to James Perkins, the man who was to lead First National out of the depression.

Born to a middle-class family in St. Louis (his father was a railroad claims adjuster), Moore was encouraged to go to college by his father who felt he had been stymied in life because of his lack of education. After graduating from Yale, George Moore took a first job with Farmers' Loan & Trust; as a result, he essentially only worked for one banking organization during his banking career. Moore played a part in the history of the bank during the troubled depression days, through its recovery in the 1930s, the war and postwar years, and the beginning of boom times in the 1950s.

When Rockefeller moved up to be chairman of First National City in 1959, it was almost a foregone conclusion that Moore would be named president. Actually, nominally he had been vying with another senior officer, Howard Laeri, but there really was no match. And there was no contest.

Rockefeller and Moore

Although Rockefeller chose Moore to be his second in command, there really was no love lost between the two men. In writing about his years as president, George Moore had this to say in *The Banker's Life* (W. W. Norton, 1987):

> ...We were in all honesty very different personalities; when he [Rockefeller] was chairman and I was president, Fred Donner, chairman of General Motors, said that the bank had a chairman who never talked and a president who never listened. We respected each other, Rockefeller and I, but I can't say there was great affection between us. He was totally lacking in youthful drive (I used to say he was fifty the day he was born), and he thought I had too much of it. When the rules of the bank forced him to retire at age sixty-five, and I became chairman, he staged a strange little personal drama to keep me from having the title "chief executive officer." He stayed on the board, which no retiring chairman had ever done before, and *nobody* got the title of CEO. It was, I suppose, a kind of way for Rockefeller

to get even, because—with a lot of help from my assistant and then successor Walter Wriston—I'd been in effect running the bank for some time while Rockefeller had the title of CEO.

...I didn't give orders—James Perkins, my first boss and sponsor at the bank, had taught me that the way to manage was never to give an order but to lead people, get them to think that what you wanted them to do was their own idea. Rockefeller was authoritarian and secretive, and if that's the way you relate to the world around you, you give orders. Sometimes you then have a problem finding out whether they were obeyed....

That passage tells you a great deal about James Stillman Rockefeller; it tells as much or more about George Moore and his leadership of the bank. Moore was opinionated and assured. He soon became known for his aggressiveness, for his eagerness to build and shape...and to succeed. Moreover, he spoke his mind, and people generally knew right where they stood with him. On balance, he also had a smooth managerial style that accomplished a great deal for him and for National City Bank.

Moore fairly jumped at the chance to run the bank and take it where he thought it ought to go. "Around 1960," he said, "we in Citibank took a new position. We would not merely be a bank. We would become a financial service company. We would seek to perform every useful financial service, anywhere in the world, which we were permitted by law to perform and which we believed we could perform at a profit."

In truth, this really wasn't a departure from the past, since it encompassed elements of the thinking of such Citi giants as Frank Vanderlip and James Mitchell.

Studying the Bank

Probably the one thing that made Moore noticed, and probably solidified his path to the top of the organization was a study he made in the late 1940s to determine exactly what the bank was doing, how it was doing it, and what could be done better. Sheperd and chairman William Gage Brady approached him with the project in 1948; the study took 18 months to complete.

At the time, National City had no game plan, there were no yardsticks, there was no profit-and-loss statement. The bank was being run on the assumption that anything that made the bank bigger would also make it more profitable.

Moore, of course, knew there was a great deal wrong with the way the bank was being run. Too many departments and divisions operated as separate entities. Even routine matters were often problems, he thought.

"We did not have a central file you could call and find out whether Moore was a customer of the bank."

Moore used the committee as an opportunity for him to push his belief in the viability of term loans for businesses. "We were helping the country build the airlines and gas pipelines and power plants it would need in the future, and it seemed unwise to pretend that such expenditures could be financed by short-term loans under conventional credit lines," he wrote. "These loans required an analysis quite different from what a traditional banker did when he helped a department store stock the shelves for the Christmas season...." Not to be overlooked, term loans paid higher rates of interest.

Both Sheperd and Brady were traditional bankers who harbored a deep-seated distrust of term loans; in fact, at the time, they had worked out an arrangement to decrease the bank's term loan portfolio.

To counter this, Moore set up a study of the project, called "Term Loan Liquidity and Earnings Projection." In a memo to Brady, the committee reported that the "liquidation of our term loan portfolio, which is now taking place and is in further prospect, may have a substantial adverse effect on interest income." The ploy worked, and the minutes of a committee meeting noted that "Mr. Moore reported that the term loan study had been referred to Mr. Brady who had commented that term loans with a maturity no longer than five years were desirable if the interest rate was sufficient." Over time, that limit was extended to 7 years, and even to 10 years in special situations.

In its report, the committee made a number of recommendations, many of which were acted upon. It resulted in a greater emphasis on profits and the installation of divisional profitability statements. But it had more far-reaching impact that helped to shape the culture of the organization. As Moore stated in his report, "Our projects and recommendations must be regarded more in the nature of a catalyst, or a series of ideas and possibilities, rather than a finished product on which a final decision could or should be made.... It was clear to us that our existence, and our work, was stimulating many to re-examine their own work in a similar inquisitive light."

Pride and Performance

One thing can be said about George Moore; he was not modest. As he puts it, "My time as president and chairman of Citibank was a period of great growth."

He is certainly right about that. At year-end 1959, the year in which he became president, the bank had $8.3 billion in assets and $68 million in profits. In 1969, his last full year before retiring, assets were $23 billion and profits amounted to $119 million. The number of employees had grown from 18,000 to 34,000. George Moore should be proud of that record.

How did Moore engineer such growth, increasing assets by nearly 300 percent in 11 years? He believes that much can be accomplished by letting people do things in their own imaginative way—within limits, of course.

In his book *The Banker's Life*, Moore places what was achieved under four headings:

1. Most simply, we got the ship in motion. We created a planning and budgeting process. We identified the potential of the overseas business, and the people we hired and promoted realized that potential.

2. We identified the financial services concept—that there was more in the life of our institution than just being a bank. To facilitate our entry into other financial services, and to give us the added stability of funding by the public sale of securities, we created the holding company, First National City Corporation, later Citicorp.

3. We constantly expanded our personnel programs, our procedures for finding, training, and promoting personnel. Without the capable people these procedures developed, none of our goals would have been attainable.

4. We made Citibank an "institution" with a clear-cut plan everybody understood and worked to achieve, as contrasted to an organization that had been to a large extent the wishes and judgment of a few people who had headed it from time to time. Citibank will never be a personal bank again!

Pumping Up the International

The International Division, long a strong suit at First National City, had been going downhill for years when George Moore took charge of the unit in 1956.

At the end of 1955, there were 61 branches in foreign countries, down from 83 in 1930. Only three of those branches were in Europe. While the overseas staff was competent and knew a lot about the countries for which they were responsible, they were getting relatively old and morale was down. Actually, most of the overseas personnel were from nations other than the United States; only a small percentage of the nearly 4000 staff members stationed in foreign countries were U.S. citizens. Promotions were rare; contact with the New York headquarters was sporadic, at best. In 1955, the international branches contributed 15 percent to the bank's before-tax earnings; in 1930, that figure was 30 percent. There was no doubt about it, the division was in bad shape.

According to a study of Citibank published by the Harvard University Press, George Moore wasted little time in breathing new life into the International Division:

> To speed change, he built a new informal structure inside the old one, infusing into this shadow organization his own enthusiasm for growth. He brought officers who were eager to become the agents of change from the rest of the bank, particularly from the Domestic Division, and added new recruits—about fifty a year—from the country's leading universities and business schools, whom he posted for training to the bank's branches around the world.
>
> At the supervisory level, Moore effected nothing less than a complete personnel reconstruction. By the end of 1959, two-thirds of the Overseas Division's supervisors abroad had been changed, either retired or called back to New York.... In 1957, Moore began holding annual meetings of senior officers from all branches. Few of them knew one another at first, and they had little sense of belonging to a worldwide team. By these meetings and his own extensive travels, Moore created the feeling of a united organization on the move. Formerly a ticket to nowhere (before his transfer, Moore once called the Overseas Division Siberia), a job there now appeared to be the way to early responsibility and large rewards.

Moore also utilized the skills of his close associate in the division, Walter Wriston, who had become his deputy. Wriston continued as head of the division after Moore moved up to the presidency. And it was there that Wriston made his own mark with the development of the certificate of deposit (see Chapter 6).

Progress and People

The George Moore era was both a period of progress and of change. The development of the certificate of deposit, of course, cannot be underrated for its impact on the banking world.

In addition, it was Moore who was in charge of the early preparation of the bank toward the automation of processing operations. As part of this effort and in an effort to improve operations, he wanted to move very fast, some say too fast and too authoritatively, bringing in a consulting firm specializing in increasing efficiency. The firm ruffled a lot of feathers and contributed to labor unrest. Actually, Stillman Rockefeller, who as noted had held on to the CEO designation, stepped in while Moore was out of the country and threw out the consulting firm that had been causing the friction. As far as Moore was concerned, Rockefeller "had panicked."

Moore also moved First National City into the rapidly growing credit card business. He engineered the purchase of 50 percent of Carte Blanche in 1966 from Conrad Hilton (with 100 percent control resting with National City). At the time, Carte Blanche was third in volume of nonbank cards, but it had been struggling.

As stated in *Citicorp 1912–1970* by Cleveland and Huertas, the Justice Department soon indicated displeasure with the purchase, talking about antitrust violations. According to the department, if a big bank wanted to get into the card business, it should do it *de novo* and not via acquisition. The bank's 50 percent equity in Carte Blanche was subsequently sold—and at a slight profit.

A year later, in 1967, First National City did introduce a card of its own, which was dubbed the "Everything Card." Two years later, it was converted to Master Charge and became part of the Master Charge interbank card system.

Emphasis on People.   George Moore realized that if First National City Bank was going to grow successfully, it needed people—good people.

He began his recruiting efforts during his time as head of the International Division. After he was named president, he intensified this activity. And he did much of this recruiting personally. He would go to Harvard, for instance, and talk with MBA candidates. When some said that they would get lost in a big bank, Moore assured them that he would have their names and he would follow their progress. He also instituted a plan whereby college students would be hired for summer jobs in order to become better acquainted with the organization and to develop their interest in banking. It also gave the bank a good opportunity to review the students.

His devotion to personnel practices was strong. Almost every day as president he would meet with some of the new recruits over coffee. Then he would follow this up with a meeting with his personnel director, discussing problems, rating procedures, and recruiting plans.

He had three goals he wanted to attain in personnel matters:

1. Always have, in house, qualified people to carry out the plans of the bank.

2. Make sure everyone is given the best possible training experience to reach his or her potential.
3. Make sure everyone gets a chance for the jobs available, and that the best person is selected.

This emphasis on personnel may be George Moore's greatest legacy. Now retired and living the greater part of his life in Spain, 87-year-old George Moore probably feels the same way. As an interesting sidelight, while president, he remarried and started another family, soon having children the same age as his grandchildren.

Without question, George Moore has had an interesting and rewarding life. He led the way for others in the Citicorp organization to become civic leaders. Moore joined the board of the Metropolitan Opera, serving as treasurer when it moved into Lincoln Center and faced serious financial problems. Later, he was president of the board, and oversaw the transition after the retirement of General Manager Rudolf Bing. He also served on the board of the 1964–1965 New York World's Fair—and resigned when he discovered that the finances were in a mess. And he helped form the Economic Development Council of the City of New York, which was involved in opening up job opportunities for African Americans and Hispanics.

He really brought Citicorp fully into the twentieth century. And he was responsible for the ascendancy of Walter Wriston. In some ways, he could be described as Citi's Renaissance man. Writer John Brooks stated it this way in the January 5, 1981, issue of the *New Yorker*: "(George Moore) did more than anyone else to create the new Citibank, the cold dazzling inventive world money machine."

6
Citi in
Full Bloom—
Walter Wriston

Many people, even today, more than eight years after Walter Wriston left the scene, have him in mind when they think about Citicorp.

He so dominated the bank, in deeds, in direction, and in person, that his shadow still remains. John Reed, of course, has been trying to fill Wriston's shoes since 1984, and maybe that's part of Reed's problem. No matter who followed Walter Bigelow Wriston at Citicorp, it was not going to be easy for that person to match the accomplishments—good and bad—of his predecessor and Wriston's impact on banking in the United States and abroad.

The son of a noted historian who had been a president of Brown University, Wriston received a classical education at Wesleyan University in Connecticut, and then a master's degree from the Fletcher School of International Law and Diplomacy—hardly the academic background for a future bank president. Following military service in World War II, he joined Citibank in 1946. He had the fortuitous foresight to catch the eye of and become associated with George Moore during his formative years at the bank. It's more than likely that Wriston would have risen to the top regardless of that fact, but it did not hurt to be aligned with the aggressive and ambitious Moore.

Overseas and CDs

Walter Wriston became chief of the International Division (replacing Moore in that spot when the older man was elevated to the presidency) in 1969. Long the leading U.S. player on the international banking scene,

First National City already had the largest overseas branching system. Wriston was determined to strengthen the system, broaden it, and build its local customer base.

"The plan in the Overseas Division was first to put a Citibank branch in every commercially important country in the world," Wriston said later. "The second phase was to begin to tap the local deposit market by putting satellite branches or mini-branches in a country. The third phase was to export retail services and know-how from New York."

Here Comes the Negotiable CD

As time went along, Wriston also determined that the bank had to do something in order to attract business customers who were beginning to desert the banks for other financial intermediaries; many of them no longer were content to leave their funds around idle with inflation on the rise. In his autobiography, George Moore described the situation this way:

> Banks had for years issued "certificates of deposit" for a given term—30, 60, 90 days, 6 months, one year. Those could pay interest under the law, and though the Federal Reserve controlled the maximum we could pay, it usually kept that rate above the market rate for money. Corporate treasurers with money to hold for more than 30 days were usually, not always, willing to lend it to the banks by purchasing CDs rather than lend it directly to other corporations by purchasing commercial paper. Banks were considered safer. But the issuers of commercial paper had a gimmick. Informally... they promised the buyer of the paper that if for any reason he needed cash while the paper was outstanding, the issuer would buy it back for the face value. And we couldn't make such promises.

Wriston found a possible way around this: the certificate of deposit could be made negotiable, which would allow the owner to sell the paper to someone else if the money was needed sooner than the term of the CD. First National City originally tried the idea in Europe, but the Swiss Bank Corporation, which had bought the first negotiable CD, couldn't find a buyer.

In the United States, Wriston was able to get the Discount Corporation of New York, a dealer in government securities, to start such a secondary market. It probably didn't hurt that George Moore was on its board.

Now, some years after the fact, Wriston is hardly modest about his efforts in the development of certificates of deposit: "CDs probably changed the banking world as much as anything." Perhaps that is an overstatement, but not all that much of one. CDs have had an enormous impact on the industry and its competitive position in the financial marketplace. For the biggest banks, negotiable certificates of deposit run a close second to deposits in checking accounts as a source of funds.

The development of the certificate of deposit, by itself, almost guaranteed that Walter Wriston would be in line for the position of president of Citicorp.

The Total Chief Executive

George Moore moved up from president to chairman of First National City Bank on July 1, 1967. Walter Wriston became president that same day. The question was not in doubt; his only opponent had been Thomas Wilcox, but without the backing of Moore, Wilcox didn't have much of a chance. (Three years later, Wilcox resigned to become head of Crocker National Bank in California.)

Whereas George Moore was feisty and gregarious, Wriston was more aloof, had a sharper tongue, and took a more intellectual approach to problems; at the same time, he was no less self-assured. With Moore's blessings, by and large he ran things his way. Three years later, in 1970, George Moore reached age 65 and retired, and Wriston moved up to chairman. Now he didn't need anyone's blessings.

Reorganizing the Bank

In 1967, when Wriston became president, First National City Bank was still structured more or less the same way Charles Mitchell had set up the bank back in the 1920s. But too much had changed—and too much change was in the offing. Wriston wanted to move the company into the twentieth century and position it so "we're faced off against the marketplace."

One of the first steps he took as president was to call in the management consulting firm of McKinsey and Company. At the same time, he set up an Organization Steering Committee, headed by Howard Laeri, to work with McKinsey. (Laeri, who had been in the running with George Moore for president in the late 1950s, had since become an elder statesperson at the bank.) Before the end of 1967, McKinsey issued a preliminary report raising two organizational questions:

1. Is Citibank organized soundly—and for optimum profits—against the separate markets it serves?

2. Is Citibank organized to provide sufficient top-management direction to its evolution as a financial conglomerate?

The McKinsey study answered both of those questions with a "no."

After a year, during which First National City also formed a bank holding company, McKinsey and the Organization Steering Committee presented a far-reaching organization plan to Wriston and the board. The plan was adopted and went into effect January 1, 1969. Citibank historians Harold vanB. Cleveland and Thomas F. Huertas, summarized the reorganization in their authorized history of the bank as follows:

> The domestic divisions were reorganized according to customer group and industry; geographical specialization was abandoned. Officers were placed opposite different segments of the market for banking services with the intention that each officer would develop the specialized knowledge appropriate to his market segment.
>
> The banks as a whole consisted of six groups plus the Bond Department, renamed the Money Market Division. Domestic banking was divided among the Personal Banking, Corporate Banking, and Commercial Banking Groups. The Operating Division was renamed the Operating Group, and the Overseas Division, the International Banking Group.
>
> The Personal Banking Group was given responsibility for the personal banking business of the New York branches. Wealthy individual customers were transferred from the New York branches to the Investment Management Group.
>
> A "worldwide account management system" was adopted for the largest multinational customers. Eventually, this became a separate banking group.

There have been many organizational changes since then, and some of the changes have been substantial, although others have been little more than changes in nomenclature. However, the scope of the organizational changes that came about at the instigation of Walter Wriston have never been equaled before or since, and they had a most profound effect on First National City and its operations during the Wriston years. Combined with the change in mode of operation that made First National City a one-bank holding company, what Wriston wrought during his three years as president can be accurately described as nothing short of remarkable.

Railing Against Regulation

Since the establishment of the first Bank of the United States, bankers have complained about the unfairness of the laws and the regulations under which they operate, which place them at a competitive disadvantage with other companies offering financial services. Such complaints eventually led to the move toward deregulation during the 1980s, although a more precise term would be "less regulation."

Walter Wriston spent a considerable amount of his time as chief executive complaining about how unequal the laws were and calling for a level playing field. When the Federal Reserve was trying to restrict what the financial services industry could do, and more particularly when it tried to impose limits on money-market funds, Wriston warned about this dastardly plot in a speech in January 1981:

> Unequal laws are a transient phenomenon, as by its nature government has to strive for equity. Modern parlance talks about level playing fields. The poet John Donne wrote: "Never send to know for whom the bell tolls. It tolls for thee." It tolled for the banks when the Monetary Control Act of 1980 gave the Federal Reserve vast new powers over the whole banking industry. It tolled for the money market funds in 1980 when President Carter invoked the Credit Control Act to impose reserve requirements on them. It tolled for Merrill Lynch when the Oregon attorney general ruled that their Cash Management Account was unlicensed banking and barred it from the state.

Beyond Wriston's marshaling of details to strengthen his point, you might notice something else about that excerpt. It has a decidedly literary flavor, something rather uncommon among the public (or private) utterances of bankers. It gives indications of his classical training, and Wriston loved to throw in the words of poets and others, often doing so even in speeches written for him by others.

Wriston repeatedly lashed out at the laws which he thought were unfair to banks, laws which put them at a distinct disadvantage to such financial service companies as Merrill Lynch and Sears Roebuck. Some of this stance of his is explored in greater detail in the chapters included in Part 3, "The Citicorp Muscle."

Capital Concerns

As noted earlier, over the years Citicorp had gained a reputation for being thinly capitalized. According to Walter Wriston, this was the way to go and, in fact, he did not believe in having too much capital.

In an interview the author had with Wriston during the fall of 1974 for *The Bankers Magazine*, the chairman had this to say about the capital of Citicorp:

> We determined [in 1969] that our ratio of capital was too high, and we mashed it down deliberately. People say our ratio is lower than

it was five years ago, and we say correct. They say it has deteriorated. And I say that five years ago it was the right number, which is
a point not in evidence, as the lawyers would say. So we say that in
the last two years—two and one-half years—we put three-quarters
of a billion dollars into the capital of Citibank, which is a reasonably
interesting number. And we will put in an enormous amount this
year through retained earnings. The object of the exercise is to make
your retained earnings grow faster than your assets.

Bank Management and Society

Under Walter Wriston, Citicorp never shied away from taking a public
stand on issues impacting on banking and on society. And his reasoning, as detailed in that same interview in *The Bankers Magazine*, is illustrative of how he viewed the world:

> The number one job of a chief executive officer is to do his best to in-
> sure the survival of his corporation. In today's value system, that
> means that the public position of the corporation is very crucial. And
> the mistake that the business community made in the 1930s was that
> they sat home and damned Franklin Roosevelt and all the laws that
> were written, and they weren't in the room when they were written.
> All they did was sit in the Union Club and say, "Isn't it awful."
>   I think that the business community now is part of our society and
> should be involved in trying to influence its [society's] decision-
> making process which impacts their own business.

Encouraging Innovation

One of the hallmarks of the Wriston years was his encouragement of
and devotion to creativity. He himself had been innovative under the
leadership of George Moore, and Wriston continued in this pursuit. If
anything, he stepped up the pressure—and the rewards—to Citicorp
people to get them to innovate and use new ideas.

In the summer of 1974, Citicorp came up with the idea of floating-rate
notes—instruments with interest rates that would change (or float) and
were tied to some other rate, such as Treasury bills. A few months later,
when he was asked if another similar issue was possible, he answered
in typical Wriston fashion: "We ran that order book up over $850 mil-
lion in five days. If in the marketplace—which I am told is in disarray,
and I'm told that nobody can raise capital, and I'm told that the world
is going to stop—we can sell $850 million in five days, my instinct is that
maybe it was pretty good paper." (*The Bankers Magazine*, Winter 1975)

At the time, there were complaints that the floating rate notes took money out of the thrift institutions, that people thought the floating rate might give them an edge. Wriston brushed aside such criticism.

"There are 75 million people with savings accounts in America and 14 million people with mortgages," he continued. "Why should the guy in the inner city in New York with $500 get ripped off for 5 percent while a guy with $100,000 makes 12 percent so he can support somebody with a mortgage in Greenwich, Connecticut? With today's value system, that's ridiculous."

Pointing out that some 90 percent of the floating-rate issue was sold to individuals, Wriston added,

> The significance of our issue is not that it floated; it's that the savings of the workingman have been allocated by government to one sector of the society. And whenever you have price controls, you create distortions. That's why I'm in favor of S&Ls and mutual savings banks getting the checking accounts and personal loans and all the rest because it's crazy to have one little barrel of money that empties whenever rates go up. It should be interconnected to the rest of the capital markets....
>
> When we came up with the floating rate notes, we knew that it would cause a certain amount of controversy.... But it opened up a new avenue to tap the savings of the individual.

Encouraging Conflict

In 1980, after a decade as chief executive, Wriston began to think about retirement. After all, one of the hard and fast rules at Citicorp was that when an employee, be she or he board chairman or bank guard, reached age 65, that person had to retire. And Wriston was going to reach that age in the summer of 1984. His strong sense of pride demanded that he be absolutely sure that the person who replaced him had what it took to succeed.

The way he went about ensuring that this would be the case said as much about Walter Wriston as anything else he did as leader of the most powerful banking organization in the world. He long had encouraged competition between individuals in the bank, whether they were vying for a job or for an account. And this is exactly what he did in setting up a race in which the winner would win Wriston's job.

He named three men as vice chairmen in 1980, and it was soon common knowledge that those three were the finalists to be his replacement. They could hardly have been different from one another:

Hans Angermueller. He was the oldest of the three finalists, but the youngest in terms of service with the organization. As vice chairman in charge of legal and external affairs, he had one of the toughest, most challenging jobs in the bank. "External affairs," it should be noted, is Citicorp-ese for lobbying efforts. With both engineering and law degrees from Harvard, Angermueller became a partner in the prestigious law firm of Shearman and Sterling. After helping Citi in the Penn Central bankruptcy hearings, he joined the bank as general counsel. He masterminded Citicorp's regulatory strategies after being named a vice chairman.

John Reed. The youngest of the three, Reed was named vice chairman of individual bank operations. His record, detailed in Chapter 10, included pulling together the bank's retail operation at the tender age of 35. Although he had never made a loan (neither had Angermueller), he knew the bank and he knew technology.

Thomas Theobald. The third contender was named vice chairman in charge of the institutional bank. He had joined Citibank as a corporate lender right out of college in 1960. With a degree in business from Holy Cross and an MBA from Harvard, Theobald was a typical bank management trainee and the only one of the contenders with what could be classified as a regular banking background. He had moved rapidly up the corporate ladder, strengthening the Investment Management Group and heading other units responsible for multinational companies and international banking along the way. As vice chairman, he was responsible for Citi's largest earning segment, wholesale banking.

The race was run over the next four years, and it was interesting to see how those in the running were outwardly friendly with each other, although individually they tried to place their mark on the bank while cultivating others who could help them in the years ahead as chief executive. Regardless of the size of the stakes, they were always civil to one another.

During the 1980s, the wily Wriston did not play favorites and, in fact, he did nothing that could have been construed as tipping his hand. It's likely that during the early stages, he really had no favorite, that he had put the candidates in contention figuring that the best man would win. However, some time later, but before the final choice was made by the board, Wriston had made his own decision (see Chapter 10). Of course, the choice was John Reed.

Wriston's ultimate decision may have been made when William Spencer, who had been president under Wriston, retired in 1984, and the position of president was open; Wriston decided to leave it vacant. This meant that whoever the replacement was would become chairman *and* chief executive officer. If the new man wanted to name someone else as president, that would be up to him.

This same sort of scenario had been used back in the 1970s by Gaylord Freeman, then chairman of the First National Bank of Chicago. He also had selected three contenders for his job—Robert Abboud, Chauncey Schmidt, and Robert Wilmouth. Whether or not Wriston got his idea from what Freeman did is difficult to say. The interesting thing is that the concept did not work at First Chicago, which was going strong at the time. It is now generally agreed among banking observers that the wrong person, Robert Abboud, was tapped for the job. Though Abboud maintained that he had performed well, he was replaced after less than three years.

Management Selection. Of course, all this is about choosing the right person for the job. In a later *Bankers Magazine* interview (January–February 1985) after his retirement and his selection of John Reed, Wriston had this to say:

> I have a management philosophy that is very simple and that is, if you have the right person in the right place, there is almost no way that you can get hurt; if you have the wrong person in that place, there is no way you can save yourself. So, we spent a lot of time trying to pick good people And, over time, I would say that the track record has been pretty good.

Life After Citicorp

When Walter Wriston retired at the end of August 1984—actually even a few weeks before, since he went on vacation and essentially left Reed in charge—he gave up the reins of power completely. This was not an easy thing for him to do, nor, for that matter, was it for George Moore when he retired. But because of the difficulties Moore had had with Stillman Rockefeller, Moore knew how important it was to just let go. That's what he did when Wriston took over, and Wriston appreciated that and never forgot how important it was.

So when he retired, Wriston did what George Moore had done. He was given a small office at 399 Park Avenue, and he still uses it today. And he is available to Reed and others for advice or whatever help he can provide. But he really did retire and does stay out of the power loop.

For a few years, Wriston had hopes of performing some kind of service with the federal government. His father, Henry Wriston, reorganized the Department of State during the Eisenhower presidency. He sometimes mentioned the services performed late in life by W. Averill Harriman, the former governor of New York State and an investment banker, and John J. McCoy, former chairman of Chase Manhattan bank. Some of the positions they held were member of the President's cabinet, ambassador, troubleshooter, and president of the World Bank.

Any of those positions would have been suitable (and probably acceptable) to Wriston. At one point, there were indications that he might serve Ronald Reagan as U.S. Trade Representative. But his success at Citicorp also produced enemies, not necessarily of him, but of the bank. The political problems were too great to be ignored, and so his highest government position to date has been as chairman of President Reagan's Economic Policy Advisory Board, and that position ended in 1989.

Since then, there have been no calls from Washington.

The Wriston Legacy

The Wriston record at Citicorp had both high and low points, plenty of them. He managed exceptional expansion overseas, and he strengthened the bank's resolve in that direction. He also persevered through some rather dark days in consumer banking, but he stuck with it until it began to pay off.

The performance figures, even after an absence of eight years, still look good:

	1967	1984
Total assets	$17.5 billion	$150.6 billion
Total loans	$9.9 billion	$102.7 billion
New income	$103.0 million	$890.0 million

Assets increased a whopping 760 percent, and net income rose by 764 percent. While all that was happening, the number of employees increased from 27,000 to 71,000. That is an amazing record. Of course, it can be said that it took the brains and hard work of a lot of people to put those records on the board. And that is true. But it is also true that if any one person made the whole thing work, it was Walter Wriston; it is difficult to imagine who else could have done the job.

As this chapter illustrates, and as do some others in this book, most notably those in Part 3, "The Citicorp Muscle," Walter Wriston was not without his flaws. And he made some mistakes, one in particular that has haunted Citicorp for years and cost it millions of dollars along the way (see Chapter 7).

Still, he was a giant at Citicorp, within the U.S. banking industry, and in the world of international finance. No single individual has come even close to Wriston as an innovator, a strategist, a manipulator, and an agent of change in banking.

PART 3

The Citicorp Muscle

If we didn't have troubles, we wouldn't have
any high-priced people around to solve them.
GEORGE S. MOORE

Well, that quote is one way of looking at things, and if you think about it, there is a good deal to be said for looking at things that way. After all, take a look at a bank with no bad loans on its books and you'll find a bank that doesn't take risks. "If we don't take risks," Tom Clausen said while he was in charge of BankAmerica the first time around, "then we're not real bankers." A bank that takes few if any risks may not get into very much trouble—but it probably doesn't make a lot of money, either.

It was George Moore who helped bring Citicorp back to some semblance of the rip-roaring days the bank experienced in those heady years before the 1929 crash. Part of it was due to the tenor of the times—when the banking industry (finally) was poised to make the most of the postwar era. Part of what he did was the result of his own strong personality and innate banking sense. And part of it, it must be said, was due to the selection and championing of his protégé, Walter Wriston. And if any one individual set the style, the pace, the direction, the attitude, the culture, the Citi way of conducting the bank's business, it was Wriston.

Although this section is entitled "The Citicorp Muscle," this does not mean that Citicorp and/or its people were always flexing that muscle in the bank's relations with the public. There were times when it just seemed that way.

In many respects, the Citi style as it developed over the years became quite pliable, a style that adapted to the needs of the moment, whatever those needs might be. As a result, the bank sometimes could be arrogant. But it also could be ingratiating, or stern, or whatever else may have been necessary to secure the business of a customer or get that customer to pay the loan. If that meant bowling over a customer or potential customer, or bullying that customer, or even killing one with kindness, that was what was done. And for a great many years, this mix of good and bad, kind and harsh, hard and soft, worked. The organization grew and outpaced the competition. It became a bank with a vitality, a ruggedness, that set it apart from other banks in the United States and throughout the world.

Oh sure, there were problems during this period in which Citicorp matured as a world-class financial organization. Some of the problems were quite serious, although perhaps not quite in the same league as the ones presently confronting the management of the bank. But they were manageable and, after all, that went with the territory. No one ever said all of banking was a rose garden—or, for that matter, a rock garden.

The Memory Lingers On

The big problem for Citicorp has been that the impression of the bank, through its policies and its people, was—and by and large still is—to a sizeable portion of the banking public that of a giant, impersonal organization that did things the way it wanted to do them. And if you or a potential customer didn't like it, that was okay; you could go to another bank.

Not that everyone felt that way then or does so today. In fact, there are probably as many who swear by Citicorp as those who swear at it. It can be assumed that such people are getting what they want from their bank, or perhaps they have had even worse experiences at other banks.

Anyway, the perception of a powerful and not always caring bank came into being during the Wriston years and to some extent still exists today. Those who do feel this way comprise a broad spectrum of people—checking account customers who were told to use an automated teller machine (ATM) because their accounts were not large enough to warrant taking the time of a real live teller; credit card holders who received calls from cold people with unfriendly voices, demanding payment today, if not sooner; individuals looking for an automobile loan who were advised that it would be necessary to put additional money down; small business people who were turned away, not because their credit was no good, but because their businesses were too small; the president of a small bank who found out his new competitor across the street would be Citicorp and that the new bankers in town would be going after his business. The list goes on.

It's true that Citicorp has no monopoly on such behavior, that a lot of this sort of thing goes on at other banks—and not necessarily big banks, either. But for some reason or other, perhaps simply because of the sheer size of the bank, Citicorp often bears the brunt of the less-than-favorable image of banking in the minds of great numbers of people.

Today, with the bank reeling under the weight of its many problems, the actions for which the organization was notorious are coming back to haunt the institution. And undoubtedly some of the people who felt the full force of Citicorp's muscle may be pleased to see the powerful banking giant in trouble. "What goes around, comes around," as the saying goes.

Still, Citicorp, during those times when it reveled in its strength, had a vitality, a sense of style, and a real personality that made the organization both feared and admired; the banking company was in a class by itself.

It just isn't the same anymore, and it may never regain that status again.

7

International Banking, Citi Style

Citicorp's venture into international banking began in the early part of the century under direction of James Stillman and Frank Vanderlip, then continued to grow during the 1920s when Charles Mitchell was at the helm. After the great depression and World War II, the international banking efforts of Citicorp gained new vigor when George Moore shook up the division in the 1950s, and it undoubtedly reached its zenith—if that is what it can be called—during the reign of Walter Wriston. With an increasingly international makeup to Citicorp's board of directors, international banking could well be a major source of a revitalization of, or the source of further troubles for, the organization as it struggles in an increasingly competitive financial marketplace in the years ahead.

Profits—and Lots of Losses

It was Wriston who gained notoriety when he observed that people and companies go bankrupt but countries do not. And for several years, he was proven correct in this assessment. At one point, in fact, the majority of Citicorp's profits came from its overseas business, and much of those profits were from loans to third-world countries.

However, the decade of the 1980s brought a change and ultimate disaster on this front.

Citi Around the World

Citicorp currently has offices of one sort or another in 91 countries. There have been good years in some, bad years in others; good experiences in some, bad experiences in others. But the international business, on balance, has been very good for Citicorp, and the company's overseas presence is greater than any other U.S. bank. At this stage there is every indication that the bank plans to continue to play a major role on the international scene.

The worst problems in recent years have been caused by Citicorp's loans to developing countries, particularly those countries in Latin America. But before concentrating on those problems, let's look at some of the other international situations and countries in which Citicorp has had a significant presence, and let's see where it also has experienced its share of difficulties.

The Cuban Connection

For years, Cuba was an important international location for Citicorp. It also was the site of serious trouble during the 1920s when the bank became closely involved with the sugar industry there (see Chapter 4).

Wriston learned a lesson about foreign branches early on from Fidel Castro. When Castro nationalized Citibank's banks in Cuba in 1960, Wriston decided Castro would not get off that easy, and so he promptly "offset" Cuba's deposits kept in Citibank in New York. As a consequence of this decisive action, Citi never lost a cent. Cuba sued to regain its deposits, but the Supreme Court ruled in favor of Citibank. Castro has no love for Citi, so no matter what happens with Cuba–United States relations, you won't see Citicorp in Cuba while he remains in power.

The OPEC Equation

The oil crisis in 1973, which saw both embargoes and massive price increases, put the Organization of Petroleum Exporting Countries (OPEC) in the driver's seat—and sitting on increasing amounts of money. The OPEC countries, and mostly the Arab nations, wanted to place their funds in only the safest banks. This meant, for the most part, that they deposited funds in banks in the United States, usually the bigger ones.

One of the prime beneficiaries of this deposit windfall was Citicorp. And no one made more of this new-found money than did Walter Wriston. Before the incoming rush of OPEC money, Citi's earnings were approximately evenly divided between foreign and domestic operations. In 1972, for example, international earnings amounted to 54 percent of the bank's total profits. Four years later, in 1976, earnings were 72 percent international and just 28 percent domestic. Moreover, a substantial portion of those international earnings came from loans to developing countries.

The Politics of Oil. All this OPEC money flowing freely into the United States began to worry some of the politicians in Washington. Could these billions of new-found dollars impact on American foreign policy? Senator Frank Church of Idaho, who was head of the powerful Senate Foreign Relations Committee as well as its Multinationals Subcommittee, which had been looking at the investments of U.S. companies abroad, decided in 1975 to look at the foreign money in the big American banks. He asked the banks to disclose the amount of OPEC funds on deposit.

"We have to know the impact of these foreign deposits on our banks," the Senator said in a statement released at the time, "and the extent to which they may represent a danger to those banks." Questionnaires were sent to the major banks, asking for details. Some of the banks—Chemical and Mellon among them, promptly complied. However, the bigger and more powerful banks—Citibank, Chase, Bank of America, and J.P. Morgan—all refused. Many of the comments were along the lines of Morgan's chairman, Ellmore Patterson, who wrote in response to the questionnaire: "Much of the information you request would involve a break of our obligation to keep confidential the affairs of particular clients."

Senator Church, who was planning to run for President the following year, decided to hold hearings on the matter. The banking lobby, which had never been stronger, put up a united front against what the bankers considered to be the outrageous demands of the lawmakers for information about which they had no business knowing. Citi's Hans Angermueller testified that if the banks were to disclose details about their deposits, OPEC might as well take their money and move it to other countries, perhaps Switzerland, where bank account secrecy was still considered a virtue.

Other big guns were brought into the fight: Paul Volcker, then president of the Federal Reserve Bank of New York; senators from both sides of the aisle; and finally William Proxmire, who was then chairman of the Senate Banking Committee. All deplored the committee's request, warning that public disclosure could affect the stability of the American banking system.

Eventually a compromise was worked out, with the banks supplying the information to the Federal Reserve on a strictly confidential basis; in turn, the Fed would only release generalized figures, and deposits and loans at individual banks would not be disclosed. The figures, which were released in March 1976, showed that the seven largest U.S. banks held OPEC deposits then totaling $11.3 billion. Citicorp was at the top of the list.

After that, the controversy cooled down, and little has been said or written about OPEC money deposited in U.S. banks in recent years. That does not mean that OPEC money is not playing a role, even a significant one; witness the B.C.C.I. bank scandal and its relationship to First American Bank and, of course, the oil money that has helped boost Citicorp's capital base (see Chapter 1).

South Africa and Apartheid

George Moore, before he became president of Citicorp, was instrumental in Citibank's opening a branch in South Africa in 1958. It is doubtful that the matter of apartheid was even considered in that decision. However, that treatment of the black majority by the white government later was a major factor in the bank's decision to exit the country.

Al Costanzo, who was in charge of international lending under Wriston, joined with his boss in declaring that Citibank's international business would be politically neutral. At hearings conducted by the House Banking Committee in 1977 on international banking operations, he stated that the bank "had worked in the whole postwar period to try to live down the accusations of Wall Street imperialism around the world," adding that "we do not intervene politically in those countries."

That righteous expression of neutrality was challenged by developments in South Africa; there were uprisings by the black population against the restrictions placed on them by the ruling white government and the sometimes violent repression by the government against the blacks. Here in the United States, groups, including the World Council of Churches, became increasingly vocal about the situation and against those companies, including banks, doing business in South Africa.

This situation escalated during the 1970s, and finally a number of banks began to separate themselves from support of the government. Chase Manhattan and Chemical, among others, stopped lending to the South African government or government-associated companies. David Rockefeller of Chase, for one, spoke out against apartheid, and his bank issued a code of ethics in 1977 that called for "strict attention to the legal, moral, and social implications of all loan and investment decisions on a global basis." In 1979, Bank of America declared that "the consequences of the apartheid policy create social unrest that adversely affects the country-risk rating of that nation." This statement was hardly a ringing denunciation of apartheid, but the bank did restrict lending to South Africa.

Citibank did not. It continued to do business there, issuing statements that argued that its banking activities were helping all of the people of the country. And Walter Wriston said that foreign policy was a function of the U.S. Department of State, and if the United States did not want private corporations to do business in South Africa, all it had to do was say so.

The public furor against companies doing business in South Africa, and against Citibank for continuing to operate in the country as usual, raged on unabated. There were boycotts of the bank by some individuals and organizations; others withdrew their funds. For years, every annual meeting of the bank was marked by statements and proposals by groups that wanted the bank to get out of South Africa.

Finally, in June of 1987, Citibank—the only U.S. bank still doing business in the country—announced that it would sell its subsidiary bank there. John Reed made no public statement, but a spokesperson was quoted as saying, "We thought we were on strong moral grounds being there, and we haven't changed our minds about that," denying that the bank was acting in response to the actions by opponents to apartheid. According to the bank, the sale of the subsidiary was strictly a business decision. There was no denunciation of apartheid by the leadership of the bank.

Citicorp's withdrawal from South Africa has not stilled the forces opposed to the present South African government and to the limited activities still being carried on by Citicorp there. At the 1992 annual meeting, for example, a consortium of groups and individuals noted that "the bank had an exposure of about $660 million in South Africa, virtually all of which has been converted into 10-year exit loans." They submitted a proposal that would require the corporation not to hold any accounts of any public or private South African entities nor to (according to the proposal) "provide any other correspondent banking services, such as the transmission of funds."

Management's position in response to the proposal was that the bank conducts no banking business in that country, makes no new credit available to any South African borrower, and has no direct investments in the country. They did recognize the bank's correspondent relationships with South Africa, but they noted that the relationships involved no extensions of credit. Citi management declared that it was on legal grounds in these activities. In its official response to the proposal of the consortium, the bank stated its "opposition to apartheid and its last vestiges." It concluded by noting that Citicorp "is the only U.S. bank with a significant presence on the continent of Africa and remains committed to Africa's economic development."

The resolution by the dissident stockholders, as might be expected, did not pass.

The Latin American
Lending Machine

The petrodollars that came pouring into U.S. banks after the 1973 oil crisis provided great opportunities for them to make even more money. With Walter Wriston leading the way, Citicorp and other banking companies loaned funds to countries in Asia, Africa, and Latin America. The loans to these poorer countries were, as Wriston and many of his colleagues at other banks believed, as good as money in the bank. Not only that, they were profitable as hell. As the Citicorp chairman put it, "'Round here, it's Jakarta that pays the check" (*Fortune*, March 1975)— or Mexico City, or Sao Paulo, or Buenos Aires.

The problem was that, beginning in the early 1980s, the checks from those last three cities started to bounce—if they were ever mailed in the first place.

The LDC Debt Crisis
in the Early 1980s

Citicorp was lending substantial sums to Argentina, Brazil, and Mexico almost as soon as fresh deposits landed on the bank's books. It also loaned less substantial amounts to other Latin American countries: to Chile, Ecuador, Peru, Uruguay, and Venezuela, and to a few more.

Then, in 1980, Brazil began to be hit with severe economic problems. Nationally, inflation became rampant and unemployment reached epidemic proportions. Worldwide, commodity prices collapsed and OPEC doubled the price of oil. Although the official debt of Brazil was listed at around $60 billion, the country had borrowed nearly $100 billion. In 1981, the finance minister, Antonio Delfim Netto, told an officer of Citibank that his country had adopted an austerity mode and would be able to weather the economic storm with only an infusion of approximately $1.5 billion of new money a month.

Wriston and others at Citicorp bought this position and pumped Citicorp's share of that amount into the country. But next year, in 1982, there was the Falkland Islands war between Great Britain and Argentina, an event no one had anticipated. Oil prices collapsed. Brazil wasn't able to get all the money it needed. Mexico, which had mortgaged its oil resources for $60 billion, ran out of money. Then Argentina, owing $45 billion, also ran out of money.

Bridge loans from several banks and loans from the International Monetary Fund and other agencies kept those countries more or less afloat for the next couple of years. Much of the spade work done to get the money in place and on time was due to the efforts of William R. Rhodes, then a senior vice president of Citicorp who was in charge of the Latin American loan portfolio. He had worked out one arrangement in early 1984 that gave new money to Brazil and seemed to be working. It was felt that Brazil was back on target with its spending and its exports. And when oil prices fell below $15 a barrel in early 1986, Brazil's future actually looked fairly bright. As will be seen, if Citicorp could ever have been said to have come to the end of these loan troubles, it was because of Rhodes more than anyone else.

Negotiations, restructuring, you name it, continued almost nonstop over the next few years. But the situation did not get better. In fact, early in 1987 Brazil again suspended the interest payments on its debt. Citicorp (and several other banks) wasted no time in putting its Brazilian loans on a nonperforming basis.

The Bankers' Edge. There was another aspect of the foreign debt crisis that was pointed out by Columbia Professor Karin Lissakers in her book, *Banks, Borrowers, and the Establishment: A Revisionist Account of the International Debt Crisis.* She points out that there was a tax loophole that almost guaranteed profits for the banks unless and until the countries began to default. As she describes it, a borrowing country would declare a high withholding tax on interest revenue and then provide its banks with a receipt. However, instead of collecting the tax, the country would negotiate a cheaper loan. Taking the tax receipts, the banks would claim exemptions in the United States (or in Britain, which had a similar loophole). The banks would profit from reduced tax payments.

That loophole was closed in the United States in 1986 with a change in the law. And it must be said that the taxes paid by some of the country's biggest banks were ridiculously low (the loophole had already been closed in the United Kingdom); and in a number of instances still are very low. For example, in 1985, Professor Lissakers reports that Citicorp paid $30 million on a pretax income of $1.76 billion. That works out to be a low, low rate of 1.8 percent. Professor Lissakers' point: the taxpayers were subsidizing the loans being made by U.S. banks to Latin America.

Biting the Bullet

Two months after the bad news from Brazil, in May 1987, John Reed faced the harsh reality of the developing country loans. He shocked much of the banking and business community by announcing that the bank would increase its reserves for possible loan losses on its Latin American loans by $3 billion and that it would post a loss of about $2.5 billion for the second quarter of the year.

This would not get rid of the problem at the bank, but it certainly would and did help. Reed thought at the time that the crisis over third-world debt would not end soon. "These problems will be with us until the 1990s," he said. Actually, they would stay with Citicorp and most of the other banks at least through 1992.

Reed stressed that this bold initiative was taken without the prodding of the banking regulators. He indicated that it had been taken solely because of the bank's reading of the situation and that it would help the bank in the long run. This was later confirmed by the regulators.

As previously noted, most of the financial world lauded Reed and Citicorp for the move. Some other leading bankers grumbled, but most of them followed suit and, also as previously noted, one end result was the worst quarter performance experienced by the banking industry since the great depression. As it turned out, some of the other banks went even further than Citicorp in building their own reserves, both in 1987 and in following years. A few even reached the point where they had rid themselves of this debilitating debt by adding to reserves and selling their Latin American loans.

Reed's actions would seem to be a significant departure from the position long espoused by Walter Wriston. However, shortly after the announcement was made, Wriston was quoted as saying, "John Reed's doing just what he should be doing. I think what he did is terrific."

Realizing the import of this exercise in banking diplomacy (and without question the high point to date of John Reed's tenure as chairman), Citicorp, in its 1987 annual report, provided a cogent explanation of what had happened since the debt crisis began in 1982:

> In the early years [of the debt crisis], commercial banks assembled financing packages to support the immediate needs of indebted countries....These bank loans were, of necessity, of short term and to governments, for balance-of-payments purposes.
>
> Such lending, however, must not continue indefinitely. In contrast with developing countries of Asia/Pacific that have avoided the debt problem, the troubled debtor nations had built up over decades inefficient, government-dominated economies based on import substitution. For the countries to resume sustainable growth, and to continue serving their foreign debt, they clearly need to undertake longer-term structural adjustment toward more open and efficient economies with an enhanced role for the private sector.
>
> The new, longer-term approach began to emerge in 1984, when the government of Mexico and commercial banks negotiated a debt/equity conversion clause into a multi-year restructuring agreement.... The country thereby reduces its foreign debt, and its debt service, while the investing party—normally from the private sector—creates new economic activity.

Late in 1984, on-lending and trade facilities were negotiated in a commercial bank package for Argentina. Under both, new money lent to a country is channeled by the creditor banks to local clients of the banks' choosing. The clients, again, tend to be in the private sector.

These facilities were further steps away from balance-of-payments lending to governments and toward what is now called the menu-of-options approach. (This menu makes new money packages more flexible and attractive to commercial banks and supports the efforts by countries to structural adjustments.)

The most recent agreement with the government of Argentina, negotiated last April [1986], was the first package primarily based on the menu approach. (The agreement included co-financing with the World Bank and others.) There also were provisions for debt/equity conversion, an early participation fee, new money bonds, and exit bonds. The bonds were the first step toward securitization.

Under securitization, a country raises new money, or substitutes for portions of its existing debt, by issuing bonds or notes. Bank creditors gain flexibility in managing their loan portfolio to the country because they can trade the securities in the secondary market.

At year end, the government of Mexico announced a securitization offer under which creditor banks could voluntarily exchange, at a discount, Mexican public sector debt for Mexican securities on which the principal is backed by zero-coupon bonds issued by the U.S. Treasury.... Securitization will become increasingly important in the international debt management strategy as we move ahead.

The report noted that Brazil had made its first payment on December 30, 1987, on interest arrears since the country declared its moratorium on February 20, adding that further payments were expected in 1988.

This portion of the annual report concluded by stating:

A key question remains whether the developing countries will keep their long-term interests in focus by continuing the sometimes difficult adjustment steps necessary to return to stable, sustained growth. With the continued cooperation of all parties—the developing countries, creditor governments, international financial agencies, and creditor banks—there should be further progress in the year ahead.

By the end of 1991, Citicorp's cross-border and foreign currency outstandings in the refinancing portfolio (Citicorp-ese for the developing country loans we've been discussing) had decreased from $11.7 billion at the beginning of 1987 to $3.6 billion at the end of 1991. There was a drop of $4.0 billion during 1991, but a good part of that figure was the removal of Mexico from the refinancing portfolio. If nothing else, the drop showed that Mexico had been steadily and successfully working itself out of its debt problems.

Still, these LDC loans remained a drag on Citicorp's earnings (and a drag on the earnings of other banks with such loans on the books). Fortunately for Citicorp and those other banks, William Rhodes was still on the job and trying to get things in shape. He was finally able to accomplish this by June 1992.

An End to the Crisis?

Under lead negotiator Rhodes, now a Citicorp vice chairman, the major banks worked out a loan-for-bonds swap in 1990 with Mexico and Venezuela. The bonds are known as Brady bonds, after U.S. Secretary of the Treasury Nicholas Brady who came up with the concept.

Under the agreement, the participating banks have the option of trading loans for two kinds of Mexican 30-year bonds: (1) discount bonds with a face value of 65 percent of the loans being replaced, carrying a floating interest rate, or (2) par bonds with the same face value as the loans at a 6.25 percent rate. The principal and interest on the bonds are collateralized by zero-coupon U.S. Treasury bonds.

The arrangement was very successful. Mexico put $43 billion of its debts into the Brady bonds; Venezuela converted $9 billion into the bonds. The Brady bonds have been very popular with investors. Moreover, according to Salomon Brothers, the Mexican and Venezuelan bonds have produced a total return of 65 percent over the first year and a half, which is better than the performance of the stock market here in the United States.

There was a third option—the banks could provide new loans. This happens to be what Citibank did; instead of converting its $2.4 billion worth of Mexican debt, it loaned additional money to Mexico.

The Argentine Arrangement.   In April 1992, the negotiating team from the Mexican and Venezuelan crises reached essentially the same agreement with Argentina on restructuring its $31 billion in debts as they did with the other countries.

Negotiations with Argentina turned out to be easier than had once been thought by the team. However, the pattern had been set and the results with the earlier agreement had been quite successful.

Brazil Settles.   After Argentina, only Brazil, the country with the biggest debt problem, remained. Again, the negotiations conducted with the Brazilian government and the Bank Advisory Committee for Brazil were headed up by Citicorp's William Rhodes.

The committee had an international makeup, which showed the global nature of the loan problems with Brazil: Citibank was chairman; Lloyds Bank and Morgan Guaranty Trust Company were deputy chairmen; and the Arab Banking Corporation, Banco Portugues do Atlantico, Bank of America, Bank of Montreal, The Bank of Tokyo, Bankers Trust Company, Chase Manhattan Bank, Chemical Bank, Commerzbank Aktiengesellschaft, Credit Lyonnais, Deutsche Bank, Midland Bank, Mitsubishi Bank, Société Générale, Swiss Bank Corporation, and Union Bank of Switzerland were members.

Covered in the agreement was Brazil's $44 billion of medium- and long-term foreign commercial bank debt as well as a parallel arrangement for 1991–1992 interest. The banks are given their choice of six options:

- A collateralized discount bond received in exchange for each bank's eligible debt tendered at a discount of 35 percent
- A collateralized par bond received in exchange for each bank's eligible debt tendered at par, which offers Brazil permanent interest relief and protection against interest-rate fluctuations
- Front-loaded interest reduction bond (FLIRB), which offers Brazil temporary interest relief
- New money
- Front-loaded interest reduction with capitalization bond (C bond), which offers Brazil temporary interest relief
- A refinancing of existing debt

This last agreement seemingly would put an end to the debt crisis that began 10 years ago in 1988 when Mexico said it could not pay the interest on its external debt. Since that time, the banks involved have lost approximately $26 billion, and there was still more to lose. As Rhodes said about the agreement, "If greed brings people apart, fear drives them together." On the other hand, the agreement could prove quite profitable to the banks, assuming things work out as planned.

But what might have happened during all those years had the money loaned not been lost? What might Citicorp have done with the funds used for the loans written off or sold at 40 cents or so on the dollar?

International Lending Ahead

The agreement on debt reached with Brazil, momentous as it is, does not mean that the economic woes in Latin America are over. And a number of experts are expressing continuing concern. Moody's Investor Service senior analyst Guillermo Estebanez cautioned that "to the extent that they still have high debt, still have a certain appetite for debt, and long-term problems like income distribution are not solved, we can't conclude that these countries are investment grade."

It does appear that Mexico and Chile, and perhaps (one hopes) Argentina, are getting close to joining the first world by improving their economic situations. It is far too early to tell about Brazil. Venezuela reached an accord in 1990 and had a growth rate of 9.2 percent in 1991, which was the highest in the western hemisphere; however, its government was nearly toppled in a coup attempt early in 1992, and there is general unrest over corruption and a falling standard of living. Peru has yet to structure its debt; at the same time, it is facing a recession, terrorism, and drugs. In other words, the Latin American region isn't out of the woods yet; there are plenty of problems to go around.

At the same time, William Rhodes believes that banks, and certainly Citicorp, have learned their lesson with the Latin American debt experience. He has stated that many banks thought the problems with the countries were caused by a temporary cash shortage, not by the structural weaknesses that were at the heart of the problems. Keeping this in mind, banks should invest in countries implementing economic reform only if these important components are present:

- A head of state who demonstrates strong leadership and political will

- A viable, coherent, and comprehensive economic plan

- An economic team that works together, not against one another

- A belief in the plan by the president, his cabinet, and other senior officials who have the conviction to stay the course

- A method to sell the plan to the person on the street

This sounds straightforward enough. But will banks examine the situation closely enough to make sure the components are all in place? Or will they be encouraged by other factors to make an international loan—and start the spiral over again? Columbia Professor Karin Lissakers says that bankers have short memories, pointing out that banks got burned in Latin America in the 1960s and again in the 1980s. She has a good point. In the mid-1970s, banks got really burned by real estate investment trusts (REITS). Hardly 10 years had passed before many bankers were up to their ears in sour real estate loans.

Could this happen again at Citicorp? You may already know the answer. When the accord was reached with Mexico, Citicorp opted to put in new money instead of restructuring the current debt. This was a great show of confidence in the government of president Carlos Salinas, and the bank has been increasing its investment in the country by opening new branches. Granted, things are on the upswing in that country, and Citi's gamble could pay great dividends.

Then again....

8
The Retail Octopus

George Mitchell was the first Citicorp leader to really appreciate the potential of consumer banking. Before his time, retail banking was not much of a factor at Citicorp, or at many other banks, for that matter. In general, bankers did not realize that the man—or woman—on the street could mean all that much business for the bank, certainly not as far as the loan business went.

The retail side of the banking business was important, but little was done to expand it any dramatic way after Mitchell's time until the Wriston era. George Moore was a superb banker, but he came from the commercial side; to him, the business of banking was basically taking care of the financial needs of business firms. Providing financial services to individuals was a secondary, although fairly significant and sometimes even profitable, adjunct to the real banking business being conducted at Citicorp.

The Rush to Retail

It was during the early 1970s, that period when the international lending business was really beginning to take off because of the influx of OPEC funds (see Chapter 7), that Citicorp's consumer banking business was not doing much, except perhaps losing money. In fact, at one point, Walter Wriston considered the possibility of getting completely out of consumer banking. Instead, not surprisingly, he went in the exact opposite direction.

Wriston decided that there was a fantastic opportunity for Citicorp to make really big money and broaden its influence if it could move into consumer banking in a major way. Technological advances were reducing the cost of consumer financial services. If only that technology could

117

be harnessed and directed, properly, it could become a real profit resource in serving the financial needs of individual customers.

Fortunately, Wriston had just the right man available to marry consumer banking and technology and make it all pay off for the bank—John Reed. Then an executive vice president, Reed agreed with Wriston's thesis, and soon he began to shake things up at Citicorp.

Working as a team, Wriston and Reed in many ways began to look at customers not as people, but as numbers. Their idea was to make those numbers grow. Unfortunately, the numbers didn't add up for several years.

Controversial Moves

During this building period, Wriston and Reed took some steps that were controversial, to say the least.

Perhaps the step that created the most furor was the mailing of some 26 million credit card applications throughout the country. This resulted in a lot of new accounts, about 5 million of them. It also brought in a great many deadbeats, which the bank certainly did not need. Until that business stabilized, the losses were astronomical. In the long run, however, the exercise in mass credit card mailings probably paid off for Citicorp.

Perhaps more than any single move by Citicorp, this national mailing of credit cards generated deep resentment by other banks toward Citicorp. "Who do those Citicorp people think they are, moving into our territory?" was a complaint often heard in many parts of the country. As might be expected, Walter Wriston was disdainful of these comments, saying that those disgruntled bankers should read the Sherman Antitrust Law, that there is no such thing as "our" markets, that those markets are open to anyone—including Citicorp.

"We are engaged, in my opinion," he said, "in the greatest revolution in the financial service business." No one can say that Wriston shied away from hyperbole.

Another step that created controversy but had a long-term payoff was the installation of automated teller machines (ATMs). For a while there was resistance to the concept, and the machines did not generate the profits of which they were capable. But this resistance faded, particularly as younger people such as college students accepted them with open arms. Even now, there are some people who are intimidated by ATMs, but that number is getting smaller every year.

A different aspect of Citicorp's ATM business was that the bank decided it would be more cost-effective to design its own equipment, planning among other things to sell the machines to other banks around the country. But the other banks didn't buy, primarily because of their less-than-charitable feeling toward the New York giant. The net result was that Citicorp's New York machines were not compatible with machines elsewhere in the country. In addition, for years, Citicorp resisted linking up with other ATM systems, which meant that customers were limited to using the Citicorp system. After all these years, that situation is changing; in 1991, Citi finally joined the CIRRUS nationwide network, expanding the number of machines that accept Citi's ATM cards.

The aggressive moves by Citicorp to build its consumer banking business during the 1970s and into the 1980s, combined with the "take it or leave it" attitude sometimes expressed by Citi employees and reinforced by company policies, resulted in bad feelings about the bank by a great many customers, would-be customers, and former customers. The "word of mouth" sometimes was too strong to print.

The Worst Bank in New York

In its March 7, 1983, issue, *New York* magazine ran an article titled "How Good Is Your Bank?" which reported on a study about the quality of retail banking in New York City. As part of the study, accounts were opened to see how long it took checks to clear. Scores of bank branches in Manhattan were surveyed, and customers, bank officers, and tellers were interviewed. Those who conducted the study waited in teller lines—and waited and waited.

You probably don't have to guess that the worst bank surveyed turned out to be Citibank. "Our testing and interviews," the article read, "found it to have the longest teller lines, long customer-service lines, the next-to-longest check-clearing times, long waits for operators to answer phones, and a cadre of too many tellers and officers who could snap the head off a Hun.

"Automated teller machines, while admittedly a natural for the Pac-Man generation, are the cheapest way to deal with thousands upon thousands of low-balance, low-profit accounts—but the half-billion-dollar cost of automating everything that isn't tied down has slashed the throat of personal service."

What's in store for the future, the article asked? "Apparently more machines for the masses and more service for CitiExpress ($5000 minimum balance in combined accounts) or Priority Service ($25,000 minimum balance in combined accounts) customers."

This concept of requiring bank customers with low-balance accounts to use ATMs and denying them access to human tellers created a firestorm in the press—and from other bankers, as well. After deciding that things were getting too hot, Citi decided to back down. Actually, there is nothing wrong with the concept, but it was mishandled, and the bank had to deal with a major setback—apparently because it never even thought about what the public reactions would be.

According to the *New York* study, "Citibank had the dubious distinction of providing us with the single longest wait (on a teller line)—36 minutes—and this on the first floor of its own headquarters building, at Park and 53rd, just a glance away from the top brass. Citibank also had the worst teller-wait lines overall, with an average peak-hour wait of 14.4 minutes."

Service With a Smile.   In the same study, the article observed that "Citibank has also been lusting after the high-balance customer, even so far as to taunt the regular peons with this sign at the end of that 36-minute marathon: TIRED OF WAITING ON LINE? KEEP JUST $5,000 IN BALANCES AND HAVE YOUR OWN SPECIAL TELLER. The pitch is for CitiExpress, which also gives you a special service number that bypasses the central switchboard. 'No busy signals, no waiting for someone to pick up the phone, no transfer calls to different departments within the bank,' coos the CitiExpress pamphlet, in the process revealing yet more nightmares in store for regular Citibank customers. Citibank is the only bank that has no direct telephone line to its individual branches."

In a section on "Innovations," the study noted that all banks try out new ideas once in a while; however, "genuine innovation that speeds service—or attempts to—is something else again." Then the article went on to describe a few examples of genuine innovation. There were no examples of this by Citibank.

New York, Circa 1992.   In its December 7, 1992, issue, *New York* magazine updated its 1983 survey and, taking a more positive approach, entitled the new study "Finding the Best Bank for Your Dollar."

This time around, in addition to several new financial institutions and several no longer in existence, Citibank did not fare quite so badly. The magazine cited Citi as having the best approach to clearing checks, gave the bank an "A" in respect to problem solving, and ranked it second in "shortest on lunchtime teller-line waits."

Not that everything has improved at Citibank. In respect to regular checking accounts, for example, Citi's price increases since 1983 ranged between 67 and 650 percent, with an annualized cost of $290.40 (as of December 12, 1992), placing it in 10th place out of 10 banks ranked. The bank's NOW checking was rated 12th most expensive out of the 15 banks listed, although Citi fell to 15th place on January 1, 1993, when a price increase went into effect.

On financial strength, *New York* placed Citibank in last (7th) place among the largest commercial banks in New York City. Using data supplied by Sheshunoff Management Services and Veribanc (a bank-rating service) as of June 1992, the bank was classified by Veribanc with the code color of yellow, meaning an equity-to-asset ratio of between 3 and 5 percent, as well as a one star rating [with the number of stars going from zero stars (lowest) to three stars (highest)].

Ralph Nader Was First

Complaints about Citibank and its lack of service and the way it operates are not new. Ralph Nader and his consumer advocacy group had checked in a decade before the *New York* magazine article with a book with the rather straightforward title of *Citibank*.

The book was the final version of a preliminary report issued in 1971. There were few shadings of gray in the report (and not much that could be classified as white, for that matter). According to the report:

> First National City Bank has a lot to hide. The report reveals not only a pattern of unwarranted and obstructive secrecy in the conduct of the bank's operations, but also serious questions of ethics and legality in the bank's management, in its lending policy, in its dealings with the people and government of New York City, in its ties to large industrial corporations, in its misuse of the courts, in its handling of trust and pension funds, and in its attempts to sidestep public economic policy.

Obviously, the report could hardly be described as a whitewash. And the authors revealed a lack of understanding of business operations. However, the report did make some telling points:

> Growth, not service, has been the hallmark of Citibank's retail operation. FNCB's striking expansion of retail banking services and volume has not been accompanied by a corresponding improvement in the quality of service offered to the individual customers. Consultant studies, commissioned by the bank in 1959, 1962, and 1970, show that Citibank's service was relatively good in 1959, improved measurably by 1962, but deteriorated sharply thereafter....
>
> The major burden of Citibank's poor service falls on the customer, not the bank; people waste their time, suffer confusion and frustration from their inability to understand the operation and cost of bank services, and incur needless service and finance charges. Particularly hard hit are low-income debtors, who frequently obtain credit they cannot repay because the bank fails to ensure that its minimum credit standards are applied by branch personnel. Consequently, Citibank is New York's largest plaintiff; within a two-year period Citibank filed over 25,000 lawsuits to recover money from debtors in default.

Remember, the Nader report was compiled well before Citicorp's massive move into consumer banking. It would have been interesting if a follow-up report had been done after the Wriston–Reed efforts to expand the bank's consumer operations during the latter part of the 1970s.

As might be expected, the bank took strong issue with the Nader report. In fact, in a rather unique response to public criticism of a corporation, Citi published a 92-page book in 1974 called *Citibank, Nader and the Facts.*

Here are excerpts from the preface to that book:

> If the speed of modern communications, in a fashionable cliche, brings the peoples of the world closer together, it also keeps many of us further apart. Certainly, it separates the indictment ever further from the defense. This has surely been Citibank's experience with a book authored by one of Ralph Nader's study groups....
>
> *Citibank,* the book by David Leinsdorf and Donald Etra, is a sustained march from prejudicial assumptions to predetermined conclusions. Though it abounds in footnotes, the book's choice of facts and quotations is guided throughout by the determination to "make a case" against First National City Bank. The authors have not expended the smallest effort in trying to reach a balanced judgment on the bank's strengths and weaknesses.
>
> As reflected in our accompanying reply, our dominant feeling is that we were used. But we also acknowledge our keen disappointment. We originally entered into an agreement to talk with the Nader study group because we hoped that we might learn something about ourselves from a critical outside appraisal. We anticipated that the criticisms would be searching but they would also be fair. We were wrong in our assumption....Accordingly, despite the paraphernalia of scholarship with which the book is clothed, in our opinion it is a shoddy piece of merchandise. If anyone else had produced it, Ralph Nader would be demanding that it be recalled for repair.
>
> Hence this short book. It is our attempt to catch up with the distortions of Nader's *Citibank.* Here you will find our general reply to that book together with point-by-point rebuttal of major issues....

An Affinity for Credit Cards

The mass mailing offering Visa credit cards in the 1970s grabbed the headlines and the attention of veteran Citicorp watchers. But the bank has long championed the credit card concept. It was not an innovator at the real beginnings of the credit card movement in the late 1950s, but it watched and learned from the experience of others, including the Bank of America and Chase Manhattan, both of which launched their own cards.

In 1966, Citi bought a 50 percent interest in Hilton's Carte Blanche card. But the regulators forced a sale of the interest. Then, in the following years, the bank introduced its own First National City Charge Service, dubbed the "Everything Card." Two years later, in 1969, the card was converted to Master Charge, the forerunner of MasterCard.

Today, Citicorp is the leading bank issuer of credit cards in the world. And even in the midst of the recession of the 1990s, the card business has proven to be good business. It has led to even more consumer banking accounts.

Recent Developments. However, the competition is getting stronger. AT&T moved in with its own card and has been performing well. Other banks, such as Banc One, which has been expanding throughout the middle west, also have been expanding their credit card marketing. At the same time, the Federal Reserve has been lowering interest rates to the lowest point in memory, but the rates on credit card loans have remained high. This has helped banks to maintain profits, but it has opened the door for other banks and nonbanks (American Express with its Optima card, for one) to lower their rates, and they are making a lot of noise about doing so.

Finally, in the spring of 1992, Citi grudgingly announced that it was lowering the rate for its most creditworthy cardholders. The new rate schedule affects about 9 million of its total of 35 million cardholders. In other words, the news sounds good, but it won't have all that much negative impact on profits—and perhaps none at all if the economy improves and delinquencies drop.

During the spring of 1992, Citicorp also announced an innovation designed to stem the steep rise in credit card fraud—putting a photo of the cardholder on the card. The idea has been used successfully in Europe, and a few banks here in the United States have issued picture cards, although on a limited basis. The Citicorp effort is the first to be done nationally. The move has proved to be a major public relations plus for the bank, and it has received good press throughout the country as well as a warm welcome from the public.

Home Banking, Again

Home banking, utilizing the capabilities of home computers that were beginning to flood many of the communities in the country, appealed to the technobankers at Citicorp. It was a natural extension of the electronic era and, since Citi was the leader, having a home banking service seemed logical.

The system, HomeBase, was on the market in early 1983. Demonstrations were held in computer stores in which IBM, Apple, Atari, and Radio Shack computers were used. For $10 a month, a customer got a basic version of the Dow Jones newswire and a home banking system allowing bills to be paid to anyone.

There were several serious problems. First, the processing system was not equipped to handle any kind of real volume. Also, it was not fully electronic; customers punched in their instructions which were sent to Citibank. But then Citi wrote out checks and mailed them to the accounts. The big problem, however, was that there weren't enough people at the time who were all that interested in banking at home. The same was true with all the other systems being promoted by banks.

Home banking was an idea whose time had not yet arrived, and Citibank pulled HomeBase off the market.

Now, nearly a decade later, interest in home banking seems to be reviving. Several banks are offering systems to customers that are much more state of the art than what was available during the earlier system generation. Citicorp is testing its Enhanced Telephone, which would allow customers to pay bills, get account information, and move their funds between accounts.

The success or failure of home banking in the 1990s remains to be seen.

Tomorrow, the World

A few years ago, a Citicorp officer was quoted as saying: "Any consumer, any customer, any household in the world is a prospect of Citibank. Our vision of the future is that we can command any business."

Is this overconfidence? Or is it simply a faith in the capabilities of the organization to do whatever is necessary to get the job done? Whatever, it was fair warning to other bankers who might be going after the same business as Citicorp to watch out for the bigger bank.

But then, look at what Citicorp said in its 1991 annual report:

> In consumer banking, Citibank is becoming recognized the world over for setting a new standard for service. The Global Consumer Bank serves 13.8 million households through 1,666 offices in 37 different countries and territories. In addition to branch banking, Global Consumer banking includes the mortgage and insurance businesses and the non-U.S. credit card business.
>
> The fundamental strength of Citibank's consumer franchise was clearly demonstrated in 1991, despite a prolonged U.S. recession, a weak U.S. housing sector, and high unemployment which dampened consumer spending. Expenses, including restructuring charges, were reduced 6 percent from the previous year, reflecting increased cost-containment efforts.
>
> Earnings were adversely affected by record credit losses in the U.S. and restructuring charges taken during the year. Other markets posted strong results....

The Citibank vision of consumer banking entails a seamless integration of products, services, and delivery systems, offered on a customer relationship basis. It is banking that is easy, safe, accessible, multilingual in many markets, uniformly delivered around the world, and available around the clock. The Global Consumer Bank is providing a demonstrably superior banking experience to its customers and creating compelling reasons for them to develop full financial relationships with Citibank.

This is the concept of "Citibanking," combining relationship banking—knowing and supporting the customer in all his or her financial activities—with technology that enables the customer to exercise greater management and control over his or her money.

The critical elements of the Citibanking relationship are the Citicard, a customer's "key" to unlocking services at over 2,300 Citicard Banking Centers around the world; the Citi-One account, which includes checking, money market, and bankcard accounts; and the CitiStatement, a monthly statement that gives a clear picture of everything the customer owns at Citibank and reports on all account activity.

Citibank not only defines a uniform banking experience around the world but also creates opportunities to transfer successful products, services, and technologies that are developed in one market into other markets.

Quite obviously, Citicorp is doing what it can, even in the face of tight budgets and lowered profits, to strengthen its octopuslike retail operations throughout the world.

Citi has the ideas, the technology, the locations, and the contacts that can help in various countries around the world.

The problem is that today, 10 years after the Wriston–Reed experiment of a broad-scale move to develop consumer banking began to pay off, the playing field is not the same. Citicorp is no longer the obvious standout among banks in the consumer banking game.

Now there are different, stronger, well-equipped players who are not going to just watch while Citicorp makes all the plays. The competition (see Chapter 12) has ideas of their own. These other banks—and a number of nonbank financial services suppliers—have plans for this business. It may not be so easy as it once was to sustain profitability in a far more crowded market.

9

Coping With a Restrictive Environment

Almost from the very beginning in 1812, the banking company now called Citicorp has presented an untamed, vigorous image to the public. And over time, the corporate culture has reflected this go-for-broke attitude, creating a rugged and restless organization brimming with confidence that has been like no other bank in the country.

This attitude and style may have reached its apex during the Wriston years, but it hasn't gone away. It is still there, although perhaps it is somewhat diminished in intensity. This mindset might be compared to the Oakland Raiders football team, which has always had the reputation of being tough, playing rough, and not being overly concerned about who might get bruised in the process. In some ways, that's also an apt description of the Citicorp mode of operation, at least during the decades of the 1970s and 1980s.

Wriston often railed at the restrictions under which banks are required to operate. He would complain that other kinds of business organizations could do just about anything and everything they wanted to in the realm of financial services without concern for such things as lending limits and adequate reserves and dealing with the regulatory authorities. There would be times when he would become impatient with the situation and look for loopholes or ways of getting around the restrictions—or doing only what was absolutely required under the rules.

Spinning Off Citibank.   At one time, in the early 1980s, Wriston got so discouraged and upset at the advances being made by such non-banking companies as Sears and Merrill Lynch, he gave some thought to the possibility of Citicorp getting rid of Citibank. While this may only have been an intellectual exercise, the idea was more than a foolish flight of fancy. There would have been a number of very real advantages to be gained by spinning off this subsidiary of the bank holding company.

Of course, the spin-off, had it taken place, would have left Citicorp without an operating bank, and therefore it no longer would have been a bank holding company. And the spun-off bank would not have been the same bank as before the separation; about all that would have been left in the bank would have been the domestic deposits.

Under the law at the time, companies owning banks that did not directly operate in the United States were not considered bank holding companies. But a loophole had been found which made it possible for nonbank firms to buy a bank and still not be considered a bank holding company. Using the loophole, Wriston indicated he would open a separate consumer bank in every state. At the same time, he said he would buy other businesses such as an insurance company and a securities firm.

Had that loophole been used, there would have been disadvantages to such a move. Citicorp would no longer have had access to the billions of dollars of interest-free deposits at Citibank, deposits that could be profitably loaned out since the cost of the funds would be zero.

Since that time, other bankers (Chase Manhattan's Thomas Labreque, for one) have threatened to change their charters or move out of the country. None of these threats have been carried out, nor did Wriston's plan get beyond the drawing board—if, in fact, it even got to that point.

This frustration with the status quo, this attitude of needing to get around the restrictions, sometimes led to some remarkable achievements at Citicorp, such as the development of the negotiable certificate of deposit and the use of floating-rate notes. On the other hand, things sometimes went the other way. Combined with the Wriston style of leadership, his decree upon becoming chief executive that Citicorp would work toward increasing earnings by 15 percent a year, as well as his championing of what he called "meritocracy" by which Citicorp managers were given enough rope and encouragement to make things happen, there sometimes were excesses. Usually, things did not get out of hand; once in a while, however, the rules may have been stretched too far and the consequences sometimes were serious.

Parking the Foreign-Exchange Position

During the Wriston and now into the Reed years, foreign-exchange trading has proven to be very lucrative business for Citicorp. It has also been the source of troubles, and one celebrated case that began back in the 1970s in Paris, didn't officially end until 1983 in Washington. While there were all sorts of accusations made against Citicorp and a number of officers, and a legal suit was brought against the organization, the case was dismissed. A great many intriguing questions were raised, but no wrongdoing was ever proven.

The Foreign-Exchange Business

Citicorp had been a major player in the foreign-exchange business almost from the time the bank had become involved in international banking activities. This business involves the purchase or sale of one currency with another. Today, banking companies such as Citicorp and other traders facilitate the process by making the purchase or sale electronically and almost instantaneously. Citicorp is the leading foreign-exchange dealer in the world, often accounting for 10 percent of the total trades.

Because of the fluctuations of currencies, and because of the power wielded by foreign-exchange traders, there is great room for speculation—and for fraud. With the awesome power and speed of electronic transfers, the scope of foreign-exchange trading is constantly increasing. And now with so many currencies in the free market, the business is booming. The participants include banks, bank customers, foreign-exchange brokers, and once in a while, central banks. Most of the exchange business is done by telephone and telex, enhanced by banks of computers and monitors that provide current data on the latest rates and blocks of trade.

Back in the late 1970s, Shearman & Sterling studied the Citicorp operation and issued a report; the excerpts here provide some of the flavor of modern-day foreign-exchange trading:

> Markets in foreign exchange are far more active than ever before, in terms of increased volume, number of participants, and locations where markets are centered....These changes have been accompanied by the introduction of new technological systems, which speed the conduct of business and the dissemination of information. Important participants are all closely linked by telephone and telex lines, which permit instantaneous access to the latest exchange rate

quotes....The result is an efficient global network through which the huge volume of foreign exchange passes. It is a transnational market that never closes, as dealers are dispersed throughout the world, trading twenty-four hours a day.

That report, in its entirety, eventually became the focus of controversy and investigation, as we shall see.

The David Edwards Case

A 27-year-old Texan, David Edwards, joined Citibank in 1972 and was placed in its new International Money Market Division. The son of a middle-class family in Wichita Falls, financial troubles caused Edwards to work his way through Midwestern State University in that city. He hit on a fairly fast track at Citi where he soon more than doubled his salary and was assigned to the Paris office as a foreign-exchange trader.

The Texan adjusted easily to life in Paris. But it wasn't long before he became enmeshed in a controversy that eventually spawned a major article in *Fortune* magazine ("The Maverick Who Yelled Foul at Citibank" by Roy Rowan, *Fortune*, January 10, 1983) and a book (*Off the Books* by Robert A. Hutchison, William Morrow and Company, 1986). Most of the material that follows is based on the contents of those publications.

As reported in *Off the Books*, not long after Edwards arrived in Europe, Citibank held a meeting in London to discuss operating procedures and regulatory controls. Because of the recent failures of the Franklin National Bank in the United States and the I. D. Herstatt Bank in Germany, the U.S. Treasury Department had decided to beef up its monitoring of the foreign-exchange market.

One of the items on the agenda for the meeting was "Parking Foreign-Exchange Positions." Parking is the term used for transferring foreign-exchange trades to different countries in order to avoid currency exchange regulations and the payment of taxes. According to *Off the Books*, one of the participants at the meeting noted that it would be necessary to do more parking of positions because of the increase in regulatory restrictions. And Rowan reported that a Citi manual cautioned that "parking of foreign-exchange positions should be kept as inconspicuous as possible."

In 1975, Edwards became suspicious that a senior trader from Belgium, Jean-Pierre de Laet, was performing some shady operations and perhaps getting kickbacks from some of the brokers with which he dealt. *Fortune* quotes Edwards as saying, "He was doing all sorts of off-the-balance-sheet deals."

Eventually, Edwards decided he had to say something about the situation to his superiors. In the fall of that year, he told his boss, Charles

Young, the area country officer in charge of France, about his suspicions that the Belgian was involved in illegal trading activities. Reportedly, Young did not seem to be at all concerned.

However, at a later meeting, Edwards was told to submit proof and a written statement of his allegations. A lawyer friend of his advised him not to do that. Moreover, Edwards was told that an internal investigation of de Laet had turned up no wrongdoing.

Still, Edwards was convinced that illegal parking activities were going on, and he told his story to other Citi officials.

In 1976, Governor Bill Clinton of Arkansas, whom Edwards had met in London while briefly attending the London School of Economics (and Clinton was there as a Rhodes scholar), urged the Texan to work as a fund raiser for the Jimmy Carter presidential election campaign. Edwards took an unpaid leave of absence, returning to Paris in February 1977, where he again became involved in the parking controversy.

Without going into all the details, Edwards was transferred later in the year to New York. In November 1977, he wrote a letter to Thomas Theobald, then head of international banking, describing his version of what had happened over the past two years. Theobald met with him, and although Edwards felt strongly that Theobald did not believe him, and said the situation would be looked into and an effort would be made to get to the bottom of things. A month later, Edwards was given a letter demanding his resignation.

Refusing to resign, Edwards prepared a 106-page report outlining what he considered were the illegal foreign-exchange deals in Paris and other European branches. Edwards sent copies of the completed report to Theobald, Walter Wriston, Citi's lawyer John Hoffman, and several others, including Lawrence Fouraker, a Citicorp director and Dean of the Harvard Business School. The report had a blue cover and soon became known as the "bluebook."

The repart crossed in the mails with a letter from Tom Theobald, dated February 9, 1978, terminating the employment of David Edwards.

Suing the Bank. Four months later, in June 1978, David Edwards filed a $14 million breach-of-contract suit against Citibank. In the suit, Edwards charged that the bank had covered up fraudulent foreign currency trading activities at its branches in Europe.

The court papers alleged that Citibank's branches in Paris, Milan, Amsterdam, London, and Zurich had developed exchange transactions with Citi's branch in Nassau, the Bahamas. The papers charged that the European branches would appear to incur losses, and so understate their earnings on tax returns in those countries; the profits would show up in Nassau where there were no taxes on profits.

After the lawsuit dragged on for about a year, the judge dismissed the case on the grounds that employment in New York could be terminated for almost any reason unless there was a written contract. David Edwards had no such contract. He appealed the decision, but the judgment in favor of Citibank was upheld.

Nearly four years after first observing what he felt might be illegal trading activities, David Edwards's role in the exercise was essentially over.

Enter the SEC

Prior to his suit against the bank, as described in *Off the Books,* Edwards had been urged by his attorney to advise the Securities and Exchange Commission (SEC) of what he felt was going on. An associate of the lawyer, Ray Garrett, Jr., was a former chairman of the SEC. He introduced Edwards to Stanley Sporkin, head of the commission's division of enforcement.

After reading Edwards's bluebook and talking with him, Sporkin decided to investigate further. Under the direction of Robert G. Ryan, the investigations included interviews with a number of Citicorp people, including Hans Angermueller. John Hoffman of Citi's law firm, Shearman & Sterling, said they would look into the accusations and report on what was found. Several months later, on November 20, 1978, the firm reported on its findings to the Citicorp Audit Committee; on November 24, the report was filed with the SEC.

The Shearman & Sterling report, quoted earlier in this section, essentially absolved Citicorp of any wrongdoing. And on the same day as the report was filed with the SEC, Citicorp issued a press release that stated the following:

> Eight months of intensive investigation revealed no pattern of violation of foreign exchange regulations in any country reviewed. The report noted, however, that certain transactions which on their face complied with local regulations could be viewed by local authorities as being in conflict with the spirit of that regulatory environment.

In part because Citi refused to comply with the SEC's subpoena for documents, the investigation did not move for the next year. Then a former investigator under Sporkin, Thomson von Stein, stopped in to see his boss. Not happy with his present job elsewhere in the government, von Stein agreed to return in early January 1989 to assist with the Citicorp investigation.

During the first part of 1980, von Stein and Ryan took depositions from a number of Citicorp officers. According to contemporaneous reports, they felt that they were building a strong case against Citicorp, that it not only allowed the parking of positions, but actually advocated that the process be used. They also interviewed Lawrence Fouraker, Tom Theobald, and Walter Wriston. Fouraker, they found, was not all that familiar with the overseas operations and had not read many of the reports issued by the bank on the matters under discussion. Theobald claimed that he had not been aware of the parking activities of the foreign-exchange traders until he read the Shearman & Sterling report.

The meeting with Walter Wriston took place on July 9, 1980. Although Ryan and von Stein asked well over a hundred questions, Wriston supplied mostly negative answers and said he did not know details of how the Nassau branch operated or how the offices in various European countries performed their foreign-exchange activities.

According to *Off the Books*, a draft report prepared by von Stein in the latter part of 1980 accused the senior management of Citibank, not just officials at the European branches, of condoning the circumvention of local taxes, exchange control, and reserve requirements whenever "they interfered with earning profits." Moreover, the report charged the bank with developing internal controls that "were principally concerned with disguising the transactions from local regulators." Not beating around the bush, the draft report said the Shearman & Sterling 1978 report "was false and misleading."

About that time, it became apparent that Ronald Reagan would win the presidential election. A transition team indicated that the SEC enforcement division would be cut and that less time would be spent on what was termed the "proliferation of meaningless enforcement activity directed at minor infractions."

Not much happened with the Citicorp investigation or the report until the latter part of 1981. According to *The New York Times*, after a series of meetings, the new enforcement chief, John Fedders (Sporkin had been transferred to the Central Intelligence Agency), although severely criticizing the Shearman & Sterling report, felt that the case prepared by Ryan and von Stein did not prove illegality on the part of Citicorp. The new SEC chairman, after conferring with the other two commissioners, John Evans and Bevis Longstreth, agreed. The Citicorp investigation of illegal foreign-exchange practices was dead.

Representative Dingell Steps In

Irwin Borowski, who had been associate director of enforcement at the SEC, did not get along with John Fedders, resigned and became counsel for the Subcommittee on Oversight and Investigations of the House

Energy and Commerce Committee. The chairman was (and is) Representative John D. Dingell (Democrat, Michigan).

Meeting a reporter for *The New York Times* in early 1982, Borowski briefly mentioned the fact that the SEC had dropped the Citicorp investigation. The reporter, Jeff Gerth, had known about the investigation and decided to look into why it had been dropped. In one story that appeared in the *Times* on February 18, 1982, Gerth wrote that current and former SEC officials were dismayed at the decision, describing it as "the most dramatic example of how the Reagan Administration's philosophy of deregulation is turning the commission away from its statutory duty to protect investors and toward protecting the interest of the publicly held corporations that it regulates."

Several other articles followed. In one, Gerth reported that the Office of the Comptroller of the Currency had sent an "unusual" private letter and report to Citibank's board of directors back in December 1980. These communications expressed concern about some of the bank's trading in foreign currencies and stating, according to government documents and officials, that "certain of its accounting and audit procedures raised serious questions about Citibank's safety and soundness."

Gerth's article said that the Comptroller's office criticized Citibank after a long staff investigation into the bank's practice of shifting foreign currency profits from countries with high taxes to tax havens.

In response, Citibank issued a statement that maintained "its written foreign exchange trading practices and procedures were basically proper." Moreover, the bank stated that four years ago it had "ordered changes in procedures wherever we felt there was any room for misunderstanding or dispute." The same article mentioned that two House subcommittees had indicated they planned to investigate why the SEC had dropped the case.

Another article mentioned that Bevis Longstreth, the most recently named commissioner who had voted against bringing enforcement action against the bank, had, in fact, once represented Citicorp and was a partner in a law firm that had Citibank as a client for many years.

Longstreth sent a letter to the *Times* proclaiming his impartiality and claimed that his representation of Citi was very limited and did not effect his neutrality before the commission. The letter was printed on March 5, 1982. If nothing else, the letter served to add to the publicity about the SEC action. This was compounded by a news release issued by the SEC, which had been stung by the publicity and decided to state its position. The news release concluded by stating that "in view of the distorted impressions created by statements in the press, the Commission would welcome the opportunity to provide a full account of its handling of the Citicorp matter before an appropriate Congressional Committee."

Pleased to oblige, the Dingell subcommittee invited the SEC to send it the appropriate documents so it could prepare for hearings.

Several months later, Citicorp sent Dingell the names of European counsel used by Shearman & Sterling in preparing its 1978 report. The bank also suggested that the subcommittee list those areas it wished to pursue.

The Hearings Begin. Finally, after several disputes and delays, the hearings began on September 13, 1982. Stanley Sporkin was called as the first witness. He explained what had gone on while the investigation was conducted under his command. He admitted that some areas could have and should have been pursued more fully, but he stated that the material gathered was sufficient to proceed further. During that first day, in the following excerpt from the hearings as reported in *Off the Books*, Representative Dingell asked Sporkin if Citicorp had a potential tax liability in at least four countries: Italy, Germany, Switzerland, and France.

SPORKIN: Yes.

DINGELL: There is potential here of penalties, interest in addition to the tax, isn't that correct?

SPORKIN: That is correct.

DINGELL: There is potential of criminal penalties, criminal prosecutions in each of the countries, is there not?

SPORKIN: That is correct.

DINGELL: There is potential here for jailing of officers of the corporation, and civil and criminal liabilities against the officers of the corporation, is there not?

SPORKIN: That is correct.

DINGELL: There is potential here of loss of licenses to do business as Citicorp was warned in its internal documents, by its people in the field, is that not a fact?

SPORKIN: That is a very important fact.

DINGELL: That is a very important fact because that could be the entire loss of earnings and the trading in that particular nation, is that not correct?

SPORKIN: That is correct, Mr. Chairman.

Several other witnesses were called before the hearings were recessed until the next session of Congress. It was during that period that the Rowan article appeared in *Fortune*, detailing some of the story. Citicorp refused to cooperate, and Wriston reportedly tried to get the editor in chief not to publish the story. After the story ran, Citicorp replied in a letter listing all the misstatements of fact, most of them minor. Citicorp then dropped its advertising from the next several issues of the magazine.

Finally, in June 1983, Citicorp delivered the documents it had been asked to supply a year before. In releasing the papers, Representative Dingell said, as reported in *Off the Books*, they gave substantial weight to the accusations that the bank had failed to disclose information about the legality of certain of its foreign currency transactions in the mid-1970s.

On June 28, the hearings reconvened with Walter Wriston as the major witness. He was impressive and cool on the stand. In a statement, he said, "Reviews of our operations in many major markets revealed we operated properly, honorably, and devoid of abuse. I am proud of our record in that regard."

Then Hans Angermueller presented a long dissertation listing the errors in the von Stein–Ryan report. After clashing with Angermueller and the Citicorp lawyer John Hoffman over who controlled the parked position, Representative Al Gore, Jr. (Democrat, Tennessee) finally got Angermueller to say that control was transferred to the branch where the position was parked.

After Wriston, responding to a question from Irwin Borowski, read a report that referred to Wriston, the Citicorp chairman declared, "That is further evidence that everything I have done in my life for the past thirty-five years says you will obey the law."

Shortly afterwards, Representative Dingell declared the hearings adjourned. They were never reopened.

Postmortem

This long, drawn-out episode was one in which a lot of reputations were bruised, and there were few winners.

The man who started it all, David Edwards, saw his Citicorp career destroyed. Several other officers found themselves sidetracked and/or delayed in their climb up the Citicorp ladder. The SEC got a black eye for seeming to cave in to political pressures. Hans Angermueller and Thomas Theobald never got to be chairmen of Citicorp—Theobald left to run Continental Bank, and Angermueller retired and went to work for Shearman & Sterling.

And what about the Edwards-accused perpetrator, Jean-Pierre de Laet? According to *Off the Books*, he left the Citicorp Paris branch in 1978, was given six months' severance, and had a $50,000 loan to the bank forgiven. At last report, he was working in a high position for an American bank in Zurich.

The New York Times reported on August 13, 1983, that Citibank had paid nearly $6.9 million in back taxes to Switzerland and France as a result of disputes about the accounting for currency transactions in those countries. In addition, the article said that a report by the directors of

Citicorp indicated that the bank would pay an additional $3.7 million to another unidentified country.

Twenty years after the beginning of his Citi career, David Edwards is alive and well and has his own investment banking company and apparently is doing quite well. He says he has no bitterness about his Citibank years, but that "It's a crying shame what has happened to the organization."

Going to Washington

A corporate policy, enunciated by Walter Wriston and championed by John Reed, was to move Citicorp throughout the United States wherever it could and whenever it was advantageous to the organization. During the mid-1980s, the time seemed right to establish an official banking presence in the District of Columbia. Of course, this was the time when the concept of bank deregulation was rampant in Washington.

Of course, the bank already had a fairly large and high-powered staff based in Washington to handle relations with Congress, the administration, and the banking regulators, and to advance the Citicorp cause. Many of these staff people had been urging the institution to move as rapidly as possible into the Washington metropolitan area before one or more of its major competitors did.

Richard Braddock, who was then head of retail banking, agreed with this policy. Not only that, he had the backing of Lawrence Small, the institutional banking chief, who had also become John Reed's troubleshooter on all sorts of corporate initiatives. New York told the Citicorp people in the Washington, D.C., office to seriously look into possible moves the bank might make in order to open banking offices that would give Citicorp high visibility where the movers and shakers of the nation would take notice.

There was only one problem: the laws in the District of Columbia effectively barred banks from any other jurisdictions from opening offices there.

It was decided, first in Washington and then in New York, that efforts should be made to determine if anything could be done to change those laws.

Making the Move

Although Citicorp has established a presence—and in certain instances, a significant presence—in many parts of the United States, by 1985 the institution could provide full banking services only in its home state of New York and in Maine. This had been unacceptable to Walter Wriston and it was no less so to John Reed. The new chairman soon indicated that he intended to do whatever he could in order to move into other areas of the country.

Among other things, this meant that laws might have to be changed and local officials might have to be "encouraged" to make Citicorp welcome. Whatever it took, Reed let it be known in no uncertain terms that interstate expansion would be a major effort of the organization while he was in charge.

After a careful look at the landscape, the Citicorp senior management decided that its first steps would be taken in the Baltimore–Washington metropolitan area.

There were many reasons for this decision, both then and today. The region is the fifth most populous in the country (after New York, Los Angeles, Chicago, and Philadelphia, in that order). The District of Columbia and nearby parts of Maryland and Virginia lead the nation in household income. Also, the region is the fifth-largest consumer market in the country, with two-thirds of the work force white-collar and service employees. Not only all that, the largest concentration of workers under age 35 are in this area.

Perhaps more pertinent to a possible entry, the District of Columbia metropolitan area was served by banking institutions much smaller and far less powerful than those in, say, Chicago or Los Angeles. It was also determined that Citicorp might find it less difficult to work with the political establishment in the Baltimore–Washington region.

The strategy was agreed upon: Hit both Maryland and the District of Columbia. But start first with Maryland.

The Maryland Maneuvers

Frank Goldstein, Citicorp's chief lobbyist in Annapolis, the state capital of Maryland, was well-acquainted with the territory. As a member of the Baltimore law firm of Melnicove, Kaufman, Weiner, & Smouce, he had been a "legislative representative" for a number of important corporations and associations since 1968. He knew who the movers and shakers were, and over the years he had developed close friendships with many of Maryland's top politicians, including then-Governor Harry Hughes.

At the time, Hughes was both popular and powerful. Goldstein decided to concentrate his efforts on the governor, working with him directly and through the state's banking commissioner, Margie Miller, and her assistant, Charles Georgious.

Goldstein asked for the governor's support of new legislation allowing Citicorp to come into the state. Goldstein told the governor that the bank was willing to make substantial investments in Maryland and would guarantee the creation of additional jobs.

After Governor Hughes agreed to consider legislation favorable to Citicorp, Goldstein met several times with Miller and Georgious, eventually drafting a measure that quickly became known as "the Citicorp bill." According to the terms of the legislation, any out-of-state bank that operated a nationally chartered bank in Maryland as of July 1, 1985, would be permitted to engage in full banking services in the state, except that the bank would not be allowed to acquire other banks. At the time, limited-service banks were restricted to one office and could not compete through advertisements for loans and deposits. It just so happened that Citibank of Maryland was, at the time, *the only limited-service bank in the state and there were no applications pending for more such banks.*

When Governor Hughes announced the proposed legislation, he also announced an agreement with Citicorp designed to assist depressed areas in the state. This agreement, of course, was designed to gain the support of members of the Maryland legislature in the face of expected strong opposition from Maryland bankers.

Under the agreement, Citicorp would buy 56 acres north of Hagerstown that had been given to the state when the property was abandoned by Fairchild Industries. The bank would tear down the plant that was there and build new facilities for its southeast credit card operations. Citicorp announced that it expected that the operations would employ at least 1000 people and that the total investment would be approximately $25 million.

As expected, the Maryland Bankers Association did voice vigorous opposition to the proposed legislation. This opposition was countered by strong support from legislators in the Hagerstown area where the economy was hurting. In fact, the state senate was so eager for the legislation that it even amended it to allow Citicorp to establish 20 full-service branches anywhere in the state within a two-year period.

The "Citicorp bill" passed both the Maryland house and senate by overwhelming margins.

How Citicorp Wooed Washington

The situation in the District of Columbia was far different from what Citicorp had to deal with when entering the Maryland banking market.

The Washington banks figured that competition from outside banking companies was inevitable. But they did not want to be smothered by the big-city banks and by Citicorp in particular. Consequently, the local banks worked with the Washington city council on legislation that would allow banks from 11 southeastern states to establish full-service banks in the district, but it would specifically exclude entry by the money-center banks.

Officials already representing Citicorp in Washington were well aware of the situation. They also knew that Mayor Marion Barry and his administration ran the city with an iron hand. Their support was essential.

The bank already had a number of exceptionally able people working in Washington, and they soon were concentrating on developing strategies that would pave the way for Citicorp to enter the district.

Lucious Gregg, a vice president and the chief lobbyist in these efforts by Citicorp, was joined by Thomas C. Gaspard, another vice president who was expected to be designated to run any new Washington bank. These two men, along with a virtual army of other officials and with the strong support of the top management in New York, set about to get the district's power base on their side.

What a Little Money Can Do

The Citicorp people quickly began an all-court press, encompassing the mayor, some of his close associates, and selected members of the city council.

Countless lunches and other meetings were held with council members who were also invited to banking functions held both in Washington and in New York. At these occasions, the Citicorp people promised that the bank would make substantial investments in various distressed sections of the city if and when Citicorp was allowed to enter the district. This strategy, it may be remembered, had proven to be successful in nearby Maryland.

During the autumn of 1985, Citicorp held a lavish reception at the Washington Hilton to kick off the District of Columbia's China Trade Show. The show was part of Mayor Barry's efforts to improve the Washington economy and to win congressional support for the mayor. The cost of the reception was estimated to have been in the neighborhood of $50,000.

One target of Citicorp's attentions was Charlene Drew Jarvis, chairwoman of the Washington city council's banking committee, who also happened to be a close ally of the mayor. She was invited to New York on several occasions to meet with Citicorp officials, including John Reed and Richard Braddock to discuss the bank's Washington plans.

Washington consultant Wade Boggs, Jr., who had a business relationship with Jarvis, was hired by Citicorp to draft a community development plan for the bank. The plan, for which Citicorp paid $26,000, helped pave the way for the successful entry of the bank into the district. Later, when the cost of the development plan was made public, reporters raised questions, but no improprieties were found.

An enabling measure was eventually passed by the Washington City Council which allowed Citicorp to conduct banking business in the district; it included elements of the community development plan mentioned above. The Citicorp effort finally ended with the purchase of National Permanent Bank—a purchase that was complicated and delayed by a fight with billionaire Gordon Getty, who had also mounted a campaign to buy the bank.

It was a tough fight, but Citicorp had made it into both Maryland and the District of Columbia. Interestingly, the bank has made little progress in its quest for a nationwide franchise since then. Of course, the banking company has had a number of other problems to face in recent years.

The Rules of the Game

At Citicorp, for some time now, the world has been looked at from the perspective of that old saying—the right way, the wrong way, and the Citicorp way.

That concept may be changing. Parking, for example, is no longer an acceptable option in foreign-exchange trading. The central banks have taken steps to guard against this procedure, and the experience with David Edwards, the SEC, and congressional hearings puts too big a spotlight on parking to allow it continue as in the past.

Working closely with politicians has been an accepted and time-honored practice which certainly does not seem to be fading into the sunset. So it can be expected that similar escapades will occur in the future.

The Citicorp muscle, effectively used, has accomplished much over the years. What it will be able to do now and in the future is anybody's guess, since Citicorp's muscle power is not quite so powerful as it used to be. This situation has come about primarily because Citicorp has lost some of its luster—and its ability to make things happen. Does this mean we will see a kinder, gentler Citicorp in the future? Unless and until this bank that was once the leader of the financial world regains some of the stature it once possessed, the organization may well be more pleasant to deal with. We'll just have to wait and see.

PART 4

Citicorp Redux

I've got you by the balls on that one, John.
EVELYN Y. DAVIS,
Citicorp stockholder at
1991 annual meeting, April 23, 1992

To be brutally blunt about it, Citicorp presently is in
a precarious position. There can be little argument that the
banking company has been and still is in its worst shape since
the early 1930s when the bank and the country were in the
depths of the great depression. Back in those days, of course,
almost every bank was experiencing difficulties, and the
government was actively trying to do something to save the
banking system and get the economy moving again. The bank is
finally making some money, but its portfolio of bad loans is still
outrageously high, its capital barely meets regulatory-mandated
minimums, the common stock is diluted and not now paying
dividends, and the competition is coming up fast on the outside.

Sure, there are a number of other banks in trouble today,
some of them in very serious trouble. However, the industry as a
whole is also much stronger today at the beginning of 1993 than
it was a year ago. In fact, a great many banks are in pretty good
shape, setting earnings records in 1992, and they probably will
set them again in 1993. Citicorp probably won't set any
records—positive records—this year; it certainly did not in 1992.

Moreover, the economy is moving toward recovery, albeit at
an excruciatingly slow pace. Not only that, while the federal
government may have spent billions to salvage the thrift
industry, at this point it is not doing much to prop up the

banking system. But the system doesn't appear to need propping up.

In the second quarter of 1992, according to FDIC data, commercial banks earned a record $7.9 billion, surpassing the previous record set in the first quarter of 1992. During the second quarter of 1991, bank earnings amounted to $4.6 billion; that means that earnings have increased by more than 70 percent. In the second quarter of 1992, the average return on assets (ROA) was 0.94 percent, the highest level since banks began reporting quarterly income in 1983; Citicorp's ROA at the end of the quarter was 0.26 percent. Total assets of the banks reporting to the FDIC increased by only $2.7 billion in the second quarter, after increasing by $5.2 billion in the first. Interestingly, Citicorp's total assets increased from $217 billion in the first quarter of 1992 to $219 billion in the second quarter and to nearly $223 billion at the end of the third quarter.

How Bad Is Bad?

Just how bad is Citicorp's situation?

That well-known banking expert and erstwhile presidential candidate Ross Perot, during a July 1992 interview with Peter Jennings on the ABC television network, intimated that Citicorp was insolvent. "If you ever take the third world loans that'll never be paid out, it's insolvent," he said. Perot did not mention during that interview that he had sold short around $1 million in Citicorp common stock. Based on the price at which he bought the stock, it is likely he was figuring the price would drop. Unfortunately for Ross, the stock had about doubled in price from the time he made his buys to when he made his statement on television. Interestingly, the Citicorp stock price actually increased the day after the interview, although it has since dropped to the $14-per-share price range in early October 1992.

Perot's comment was almost immediately refuted by the comptroller of the currency, who usually maintains a silence about such things. And a few days later, John Reed, also breaking a silence, emphatically stated in response to a question at a meeting, "We are demonstrably not insolvent."

Not that Perot has been the only one making disparaging remarks about the financial condition of the nation's largest bank; there have been periodic declarations of insolvency made, usually by nonbankers. Congressman John Dingell stated a year ago that Citicorp was "technically insolvent." And Congressman Henry Gonzalez (Democrat, Texas), who is the chairman of the

House Banking Committee, suggested last year that it might be a good idea to just declare Citicorp insolvent, split up the assets, and move forward from that point.

The thing is, figures can be stacked to back up any stand one wishes to take. As our friend Paul Nadler once asked, "Should bank annual reports be placed in the fiction section of the library?" His implied answer, of course, was "yes."

So if one looks closely at the performance results issued by Citicorp at the end of the second quarter of 1992, it is difficult to determine how much fiction is in the report. And it is possible to stack the figures to give the impression, at least, that Citi is technically insolvent, or perhaps was at some point in 1991 when the Congressmen made their statements. Incidentally, Representatives Dingell and Gonzalez were not willing to repeat those comments for this book—not that the financial data has changed all that much, because it hasn't.

Besides, no matter what, the regulators and the federal government are not about to let a bank the size of Citicorp fail. Remember, they did just about everything they could to keep Continental Bank afloat. If Citi was at the point Continental was in the mid-1980s, you can bet the ranch the government would do far more to prop up the nation's largest bank. And in as bad a shape as it is, Citicorp is not even close to where Continental was when the regulators stepped in.

The banking regulators monitor the condition of banking companies under their jurisdictions. And the FDIC maintains a list of what are called "problem" banks, institutions with financial, operational, or managerial weaknesses that threaten their financial viability. As of June 30, 1992 (the most current figures available), there were 956 "problem" banks; this is 8.18 percent of the 11,685 commercial banks reporting; the assets of the problem banks amounted to $494 billion. The specifics of the problem banks are kept extremely confidential by the federal regulators. The regulators assign a rating to each financial institution, based upon an evaluation of financial and operations criteria. The rating is set on a scale of 1 to 5 in ascending order of supervisory concern. Depending on the degree of risk and, therefore, supervisory concern, the problem banks are rated either a 4 or a 5.

Is Citicorp considered a problem bank by the regulators? It is impossible to say for certain one way or the other, although admittedly its performance over the past couple of years has not been good. However, it should be pointed out that even if it was a 4 or 5, that does not mean the bank is insolvent or even is in danger of failing. Many banking companies that find themselves

on the list can and do get off and then become successful
organizations again; one of the best examples is BankAmerica,
which was in deep trouble during the mid-1980s and now is in
the process of mounting a serious challenge to Citicorp as the
largest bank in the country.

Back to Reed

Citicorp today is, in large measure, what the leadership of John
S. Reed, chairman and chief executive officer, has made it. He
has run the company for eight years now, and the depressed
condition of the bank today is his responsibility because it has
happened on his watch.

Although Reed is officially accepting this responsibility, there
are some indications that he is beginning to blame the bank's
condition on what occurred before he came to power. Certainly,
some of the problems, such as the third-world loans, can be
traced back to Walter Wriston. And John Reed can take credit
for handling that problem perhaps as well as it could be
expected to be handled. However, Reed has had the time, as well
as the opportunity, to make what changes might be necessary in
other areas of the company, including those he has complained
about. His complaints sound something like George Bush
saying, in the campaign of 1992, that the current problems
facing the country were all Jimmy Carter's fault.

To know Citicorp today, then, is to know Reed—his strong
points, his weak ones, his managerial style, his successes, his
failures. And that is where we begin this final section of the
book.

10
John Reed—
Man and Manager

The board of directors of Citicorp met in a special session on June 19, 1984, at 4 p.m. to elect a new chairman and chief executive officer. He would succeed Walter Wriston, who would retire at the end of August after reaching the age of 65, the corporation's mandatory retirement age. The meeting was supposed to be heavy with suspense, with the entire financial world waiting breathlessly. In fact, the decision had actually been made at least a year and a half before, when Wriston told the board's personnel committee that he wanted John Reed to have the position.

The official announcement was delayed until the morning of June 20 so the bank could inform its thousands of employees worldwide. Actually, Reed had inadvertently let the cat out of the bag in early May during a speech at the American Bankers Association Operations and Automation Conference in Washington, D.C., when he said he would do something "after he became chairman." Surprisingly, no one attending his presentation, including several members of the press, picked up on this statement.

From the publicity generated by the retirement of Wriston and the elevation of Reed, you would have thought the financial world was getting a new pope. However, the publicity served to dramatically demonstrate the importance of Citicorp and the stature Walter Wriston had gained in the world of banking. Moreover, overnight John Reed became the most important banking star in the firmament.

The Making of a
Technocratic Banker

In some ways, John Shepard Reed did not seem a likely candidate for a career in banking; in fact, he had never been a banker in the traditional

147

sense. But then, the board was not really looking for that kind of banker; they wanted a manager. Even more than that, the Citicorp directors wanted a manager who was comfortable with the new technology that was redefining the banking industry. And if that individual also had played a major leadership role in the rapidly blossoming flagship of Citicorp's business, retail banking, so much the better. As it turned out, John Reed seemingly was ideally suited to the managerial needs of the organization in 1984.

Reed, who was born in Chicago in 1939, was raised in South America where his father was a plant manager for Armour and Company. Except for two years when the family lived in São Paulo, John Reed spent his youth in Buenos Aires. He went to the American school there and became fluent in both Spanish and Portuguese. He received undergraduate degrees from Washington and Jefferson College and the Massachusetts Institute of Technology (in physical metallurgy). After serving with the Army Corps of Engineers in Korea, and then a year as a systems analyst for Goodyear Tire and Rubber, Reed went back to school. He earned an M.S. at M.I.T.'s Sloan School of Management, where he was recruited by Citicorp, joining the bank in 1965.

His first job at the bank was as a planner in the International Division, then headed by Walter Wriston. This was followed by an assignment in the operations group, in which he helped to solve growing back-office problems that were plaguing the bank. He worked for William Spencer, who was then named president; when Spencer moved up, Reed took over as head of the group.

Reed was able to solve problems where others had failed because he did not try to apply computers to traditional operational problems; instead, he looked at reshaping the functions of the division so the group could take advantage of the cost- and time-saving potential of the new technology. His efforts later were used as a Harvard Business School case study on curbing escalating costs and dealing with mounting errors. In the study, Reed was quoted as saying his approach was to view the bank's computer center as a "factory, a high-speed, continuous-process production operation." However he viewed it, he broke up the operation into manageable, controllable, understandable pieces. And it worked.

His efforts with the operations group were what made Reed's name at the bank and virtually assured him of a bright future at Citicorp. George Moore characterized this phenomenon by saying that when John Reed adjusted the bank's operations to computers, he got "sufficient velocity from it to propel him all the way to the chairman's slot after Wriston retired."

The budding banker was also lucky in having not one, but two mentors watching over him. Walter Wriston, in the long run, proved to be the most valuable. At the same time, he got a big boost from William Spencer. With the help of Wriston and Spencer, Reed could hardly have been on a faster track.

At the same time, the methods he employed in operations, which included such moves as slashing payrolls and issuing guidelines without explanations, did not win him many friends among staff members. These employees gave him a nickname to which he was often referred behind his back, one that traded on his boyish looks: "the Brat."

Focusing on Consumer Banking

That nickname did not deter Walter Wriston, who fully appreciated Reed's accomplishments. Then, in the mid-1970s, Wriston decided that Citi should be a leader in providing financial services to consumers. He selected Reed to head up a major move into this field. Included in the services being promoted would be such potentially profitable activities as expanding home mortgage lending, blanketing the country with millions of unsolicited applications for Visa cards, and pioneering the use of ATMs, particularly in the New York City metropolitan area.

The effort, ambitious though it was, did not prove to be an overnight success.

In fact, for six years the effort cost the bank a small fortune; the bad debts from the credit card solicitation alone were written off to the tune of $80 million. Fortunately, other units of the bank were making enough money to more than cover the losses. Eventually, the division solved its problems, and it began to make money—big money. Both Wriston and Reed came out winners for having the vision to move in the consumer banking direction and the perseverance to stay with the program until success was attained.

The Workaholic

During his early days at Citicorp, and particularly when he was head of the operations group, John Reed spent increasing amounts of his time at work. The long hours must have left little time for his family. He also traveled a great deal, often being away from home for several days at a time, further increasing his level of job stress. At the office, the strain was beginning to show: Reed was often curt with his subordinates, seemingly unconcerned about the feelings and needs of others. For several years he had a reputation as a somewhat cold taskmaster, and he had few friendships within the bank because of the way he dealt with both subordinates and with his peers.

In the mid-1970s, however, he apparently experienced some kind of metamorphosis, and he dramatically altered his lifestyle. No longer did he stay at the office until midnight; instead, he returned to his suburban home around six in the evening like a normal commuter (although he often could be found in his office as early as five in the morning). Anyway, his crisis passed.

The change at the office was very noticeable. He became much more friendly, not turning off people nearly as often with a stare or a cutting remark. His associates describe the change as "abrupt" as well as most welcome, and one officer said Reed actually became people-oriented. Had the change not occurred, many observers of the Citi scene do not think Reed would have been named one of the three contenders for Wriston's job, and he certainly would not have been named the winner.

After this behavior change, in the late 1970s, Reed and his family appeared in a series of advertisements for *Scientific American*, which happened to be one of his favorite magazines, and one he still reads. In one of the ads he was shown on a sailboat, dressed in leisure clothes, the epitome of a young, good-looking, and obviously successful banker at play. The caption read: "The Citi is banking on John Reed for the future." How did they know?

The advertisements created quite a furor at Citicorp headquarters. Some people within the organization were less than pleased. Moreover, it seemed to be so out of character for him to have agreed to appear in the ads. But it did help to show that beneath his cool business demeanor, John Reed was a regular guy after all. And the ads probably did not hurt the image of Citicorp, either.

(More recently, there have been rumors of another family crisis. However, you will not read the details in this book; if you are really interested, you might check the gossip columns in the tabloids.)

Tough Man in a Tough Job. Someone said that the change that took place in John Reed in the mid-1970s was almost as if he had gone to charm school. Perhaps, but that does not mean he graduated.

There are some people today who describe the Citicorp chairman as insensitive, unthinking, at times abrasive. Perhaps like all of us, he has his good days and his bad days. With the current state of his bank's business, the bad days may be occurring with greater frequency.

When he decided to move the executive offices from the fifteenth to the second floor of 399 Park Avenue to encourage a collegial atmosphere, Reed had his office built with glass walls. This means that people on that floor near his office can look in and see their chairman hard at work, usually with his suit coat off and his shirt-sleeves rolled up.

That does not mean that they can walk right in. One can see through the walls, but the walls are still there.

Taking Command

When John Reed actually took over as chairman of Citicorp on September 1, 1984, he became chief of the biggest, strongest, most powerful bank in the world. The organization was feared by many and respected by many more, and it was the business enemy of more than a few. J. Richard Fredericks, bank analyst for the San Francisco firm of Montgomery Securities, described the organization this way: "There are hardly any banks—and few companies—that can be compared to Citibank for sheer size and power."

But all was not serene; there were problems. The third-world debt crisis was already causing reverberations at 399 Park—Citicorp had over $12 billion in loans to six Latin American countries that were in deep economic trouble. The stock was trading in the neighborhood of $30 per share, far below the $46 it was selling at just a year before.

Looking at the situation at the time of Reed's ascendancy, Anthony M. Santomero, professor of finance at the Wharton School, pointed out that among other things there were two different cultures in conflict at Citicorp—one, the corporate (traditional) bankers who were being shunted aside, or so they thought, by the other, technobankers working for consumer banking: "One of John Reed's jobs will be to integrate the corporate and the retail side. Corporate banking is very large and very aggressive. And if it is not receiving the right kind of attention, this is likely to cause concern. One of the things Mr. Reed will have to do is make evident his commitment to the entire bank."

What the professor was describing was the kind of human problems that many doubted Reed was capable of handling. However, Irving Shapiro, the former head of Du Pont and a member of the Citicorp board that elected John Reed chairman, had no doubts about Reed's capabilities, stating that he had "great capacity for conceptual thinking, has enormous intellectual power, and is a very bright man. Despite what I read, he relates well to his troops...."

On the technology side, there were few, if any, who doubted Reed's capabilities. Banking analyst George Salem, who is now with Prudential Securities, stated then that "John Reed is probably the number one banker in America in terms of knowledge and experience in applying technology to the financial services business. Electronics is vital. It's the linchpin that makes Citicorp different from the others and gives them the edge in efficiency."

Of course, as will be seen, efficiency isn't everything.

The Delta Force

Reed's first move really was not his, and it actually began in August 1984, *before* he was officially in charge. However, since Wriston would be going on vacation, the decision to put Operation Delta, as it was called, into effect was up to Reed and he authorized it. Delta was a plan in which 2500 Citicorp officers were asked to find ways to cut costs by as much as 40 percent by the end of the year.

The plan was unexpected and not particularly welcomed by staff members. This was understandable, since reducing expenses by such an amount would naturally require significant reductions in the number of employees; not that Citicorp hadn't grown a little fat or that similar plans weren't in place at other banks, including such local competition as Bankers Trust and Chase Manhattan. As it turned out, the number of employees at Citicorp kept increasing, from 71,000 at the end of 1984 to 81,000 at year-end 1985, and up to 88,500 in 1986.

It was pointed out by some bank officials that the true objective of Operation Delta was not so much cutting costs as it was a means of instituting a disciplined approach to the establishment of priorities. As such, it may or may not have accomplished its objectives. The plan was illustrative of the mindset of John Reed. No one really should have been surprised; even if he had been chief executive at the time the plan was suggested, chances are that it would have had his approval. And it did effectively demonstrate that Reed was determined to start fast and that this could well be the beginning of an activist administration by the newly elected chairman, John Reed.

But it wasn't.

An official of a competing bank said that if you closed your eyes, "you wouldn't know whether Wriston or Reed was running the show." That was because at the beginning, Reed adhered closely to Wriston's policies and procedures; there were few, if any, changes. However, in other ways, Reed operated with a much lower profile, and for the most part he did not make as many or as high waves as did the man he replaced.

In fact, as already indicated in Chapter 3, Reed moved relatively slowly, particularly in getting his own senior management team in place. As it turned out, for the most part, Reed's reign was slow, steady, deliberate—and less than spectacular.

A Billion-Dollar Year

At the same time, a good deal was accomplished during Reed's early years as chairman.

Even with two different chairmen and a change in administrations, 1984 was a vintage year for Citicorp, better than had been expected.

And the long-time goal of earning a billion dollars in one year could have been reached in 1985. That year, profits amounted to $998 million. In an organization the size of Citi, $2 million easily could have been taken from write-offs of bad loans to make up the difference and not even have been noticed. Chances are, Wriston would have done something like that, and he would have provided the organization with a great public relations plus in the process. It certainly would have been a feather in John Reed's cap. Instead, Reed sought to show a conservative bent, adding to reserves, investing in long-term projects, and perhaps trying not to overshadow Wriston too soon.

As it turned out, he was given high marks by many analysts and bankers for not going for the record and instead indicating a willingness to build for the future. And there was plenty of building going on. Assets increased in 1985 by $23 billion to $174 billion. Acquisitions soared, both here and abroad. The bank even opened an office in Beijing.

Reed also tried to keep the old team together and did rather well, particularly in holding on to former rival Tom Theobald (see Chapter 3). In addition, he promoted some of his close allies, such as Richard Braddock and Lawrence Small.

While doing all this, he consciously kept a low profile, something Wriston never tried to do. Almost without exception, Reed declined to be interviewed. (Even when he was elected chairman, he only made a brief formal speech and deliberately stayed clear of the press.) Reed rarely made the kind of policy statements Wriston relished making about the banking industry. He was content to let his actions and Citicorp's performance speak for him. For the first couple of years, that was more than enough.

Leading the Industry

Not only did John Reed shy away from interviews, he rarely made statements to the press. Most of the impressions the outside world got of Reed were from his meetings with bank stock analysts—and in the beginning the signals received were decidedly mixed. At an August 1986 meeting with analysts, he discussed in detail the long-term prospects for the bank. When asked about the short-term situation, he would go back to discussing the long-term outlook. Reed then engaged in a limited debate with some of his associates about short-term earnings in front of the audience of analysts. This public display of dissension was viewed with disbelief by the analysts—and the price of the stock briefly tumbled.

In yet another departure from the Wriston style, Reed did not even try to pretend to speak for the banking industry about the problems facing banking in the United States.

That is, he did not until he moved forcefully and quite dramatically to put a halt to the hemorrhaging that was occurring at many banks because of the defaults on loans to third-world countries, to several Latin American nations in particular. Citicorp had led the way to South America and had, by example and with exceptional profits, encouraged other banks to go in the same direction. When the loans were not repaid, Citicorp was hit the hardest because its exposure was the greatest.

The Citicorp move to set aside reserves to help cover its deteriorating Latin American loan portfolio is described in Chapter 7. A great many banks followed the Citi lead. (One notable exception, at first, anyway, was BankAmerica, which had many other problems at the time.)

This bold step marked the first time that John Reed had taken decisive action, at least in such a public way. And for the first time, it showed the industry that Reed was capable of playing a leading role on the banking scene. He was willing to absorb a huge hit that would decimate profits and, in fact, lead to an almost unbelievable single-year loss for Citicorp in 1987. Most of the other banks that followed his lead also posted substantial losses that year. As a consequence, the industry as a whole, had one of its worst years in terms of profits since the great depression.

Did this Latin American loan action signify a change on the part of John Reed? Would this lead to more interviews, to more efforts to speak for the industry in both public and private forums? Apparently not. At least for the time being, it turned out to be a one-time deal.

A Selective Audience.   One of the first full-fledged, in-depth interviews given by John Reed appeared in the November–December 1990 issue of the *Harvard Business Review*. While a fine publication, it is hardly required reading in the banking industry or, for that matter, in most other industries. Moreover, he was not interviewed by a banking journalist, but by Noel Tichy, a professor at the University of Michigan's School of Business Administration, and by Ram Charan, a consultant specializing in global business strategies.

Be that as it may, it was an interesting interview, concentrating as might be expected on Citicorp's global business. John Reed admitted to mistakes (something his predecessor was loath to do), and he was candid about them. He also admitted he had waited too long before taking action in such areas as the troubled real estate loan portfolio. At the same time, he gave the impression of being someone who was on top of things, who was concerned more about the long haul than about short-term results.

In that interview and in others before and since, John Reed has exhibited a refreshing candor and a willingness to accept blame. This is not a common attribute in the business world—and certainly it was not one of Walter Wriston's.

Reed reinforced (perhaps "rebuilt" is a better word) his stature as the chief executive of the country's largest bank. He seemed reasonable and informed, with solutions at hand to take care of the problems. Perhaps that was what he wanted to accomplish. And the interview received a good play among the academics and other intellectuals. But what about the people running the real world of banking? Didn't he want to speak to them—or for them?

Apparently he did not. John Reed has given only a few extensive interviews during his years as Citicorp chairman. Perhaps the first appeared in *The New York Times Magazine* in 1989. There was an interview that appeared in *Manhattan, inc.* in 1990, and an interview of sorts in *New York* magazine in February 1992. But for most of the magazine and newspaper pieces about Reed, you'll see a line that reads, "Mr. Reed refused to be interviewed for this article." So he did not personally contribute to a major article on Citicorp in the January 14, 1991, issue of *Fortune*, or in *Business Week*, or in the *American Banker* newspaper, or in any of the banking magazines—or, for that matter, for this book.

Rebound and Fall Back

After the 1987 effort to control the Latin American debt problem and the resulting loss of over $1 billion for the year, Citicorp came roaring back in 1988 with a profit of $1.858 billion, the most money it had ever made—the most money any U.S. bank had ever made.

While there certainly were bright spots during the year (there was a big jump in net interest revenue), the major reason for the show of profits was a reduction in the provision for possible loan losses, from $4.410 billion in 1987 to $1.330 in 1988. That amount was less than what had been set aside in 1986, and it was about equal to the amount set aside in 1985. Apparently John Reed was now willing to do what was necessary to make the bottom line look good. What a difference three years make!

In 1989, profits dropped to $489 million. Net interest revenue decreased, but total revenue increased. The Latin American loans continued to cause trouble, and the reserves for possible credit losses doubled from the 1988 figure.

The following year, 1990, the results indicated rather strongly that there was, in fact, trouble ahead. Profits fell by some $40 million for the year—but they had fallen by over $300 million in the fourth quarter, wiping out what would have been far higher profits. Total revenues increased, but so did the provision for possible loan losses and operating expenses. Not only that, but the number of employees ballooned, to a record high of 95,000 here and abroad.

The big drop was in assets, from Citicorp's historic high of $230 billion in 1989 to just under $217 billion in 1990. Part of the drop was due to a $7 billion decrease in deposits. Yet little was made of the asset loss in the annual report, except for Reed's statement noting the "global adjustment in asset values" and "the drop in U.S. real estate values." Assets had grown steadily during the Reed years (they totaled $159 billion in 1984). This was the first decrease in many years.

A Time to Act

Without question, 1991 was one of John Reed's worst years. It wasn't very good for Citicorp, either.

The year started out bad and went downhill from that point. After finally accepting the need to increase capital, Reed sold over a billion dollars worth of a costly issue of preferred stock to a Saudi prince and an investor group (see Chapter 1). Although this move helped boost capital, it also drew the wrath of many stockholders who saw their ownership in the company diluted.

The real estate loans continued to worsen. Robert Campeau and his Federated Stores (among others) went bankrupt, leaving Citicorp with more bad debts. After the disastrous third-quarter loss, the quarterly dividend was eliminated (after having been reduced at the beginning of the year). At year-end, there was a loss of $457 million, loan loss reserves increased, and assets decreased slightly. The consumer bank made a profit of more than half a billion dollars, but that was far less than what it made in 1990. About the only positive note was that the number of employees had dropped to 86,000, a decrease of 9000 within the past year; obviously, the steps taken to reduce costs were beginning to take effect.

Making a Move. At the beginning of the year, John Reed began a program designed to stop Citicorp's free fall and (it was hoped) turn things around. His five-point program— (1) focus on the short term, (2) reduce costs, (3) strengthen capital, (4) build on the bank's core businesses, and (5) focus on the customer—could only be as good as the efforts to carry it forward.

Fortunately for Citicorp and for John Reed, steps have been and are being taken to get the company moving in the right direction. This has, among other things, involved a dramatic break with the past in the matter of capital. As a management memo to Citicorp employees in December 1990 stated: "The notion of low capital balanced by a broadly diversified business is simply not accepted in today's world."

Further reductions in the number of employees took place during 1992, bringing the total down to approximately 80,000 employees worldwide at the beginning of 1993. In addition, operating costs (which, of course, include personnel) have already been lowered to $9.4 billion a year, down from $11 billion in 1990; Citi expects to be at or below the $9 billion mark by the beginning of 1993.

The 1992 Annual Meeting

Based on the 1991 performance, it might have been expected that there would be an overflow crowd at the Citicorp annual meeting, held April 23, 1992, in the auditorium at 399 Park Avenue. In fact, the room was not full, although Citi officials had been prepared for many more people.

Not only that, by and large the crowd was almost docile. The only people on the stage were John Reed and Charles R. Long, executive vice president and secretary of the holding company. The board was seated in the first row.

There were few comments by other than the usual group of corporate gadflies—John Gilbert (his brother Lewis was ill), Evelyn Y. Davis, Theodore Cole, etc. And for the most part, these people stayed within the bounds of civility and good taste. Of course, Evelyn Davis did tell of her grip on Reed (see quote at the introduction to Part 4). Her comments were the result of Reed's answer to her question about lending to politicians. He said that that had no bearing on loans made or any other services extended to individuals. Then she noted (with a dramatic choice of words) that a former politician and official in the Carter administration had enjoyed a very large balance on his Citibank credit card.

For the most part, Reed was in control, which is as it should be; after all, this was the eighth annual meeting he had run. The questions were mostly "softballs," even the majority of those from the gadflies. Only once did Reed lose his cool, when one unhappy stockholder kept harping on not receiving answers to complaints lodged a year ago. Reed suggested that if that were the case, the stockholder should sue. At that point, it appeared that most of the audience was on Reed's side.

There was little discussion about Reed's compensation (currently $1.2 million per year), which is understandable. It is the lowest of any of the top executives at the five largest banks. At the same time, *Business Week*, in its Executive Compensation Scoreboard rating pay versus corporate profit, gives Reed and Citicorp a 5 rating, which is the bottom of the scale. Interestingly, Richard Kovacevitch, who is now president of Norwest, is ranked higher and earns more than John Reed.

At the same time, it seemed that Reed expected he would have been given a rougher time. As a consequence, he probably was not as smooth as he might have been. He also was undoubtedly relieved that the meeting concluded without any major flare-ups and that he had escaped relatively unscathed.

Facing the Facts

The big problem—and the one that can be expected to hurt for some time to come—is Citicorp's troubled real estate portfolio.

John Reed admits that he was warned about the real estate problem as early as 1988, but he did little or nothing about it at the time. Now, he admits that he should have acted sooner. But then, he should have acted sooner on a lot of things. Why he didn't is anyone's guess.

Even today, after Citicorp has pumped up its capital, substantially cut costs, and sold a number of assets, its reserves for bad loans, on a percentage basis, are still lower than for most of the top 50 banks in the country. As a result, the loan portfolio will continue to be a drag on earnings—and the bank's hoped-for turnaround.

A Summer of Discontent. On August 14, 1992, in a 10-Q filing with federal regulators, Citicorp revealed that the banking regulators had required the bank to restate its second-quarter earnings to a net income of $143 million, down from the $171 million reported several weeks earlier.

According to the filing, "management and its independent auditors agree that the previously reported earnings were consistent with Generally Accepted Accounting Principles, but that the $28 million adjustment of net income reflects the regulators' preference rather than management's judgment on the level of future prepayments of mortgages."

In effect, the government said that Citicorp had overstated the value of its mortgage-servicing unit that collects homeowner payments. Falling interest rates and start-up costs of replacement mortgages had lowered earnings expectations of the unit.

Three weeks later, in early September, the financial press reported that a preliminary report had been issued by the office of the comptroller of the currency that was highly critical of the management of Citicorp Mortgage, Inc. (CMI), a Citicorp unit based in St. Louis and one of the largest issuers of home mortgages in the country.

According to the OCC report, CMI had negative $80 million of capital at the end of 1991. Among other things, the report noted that CMI's delinquency rate on mortgages was 12.74 percent, four times the industry average, which is in the 3.0 percent range. Citicorp disputed the accuracy of the comptroller's memorandum dated August 18, 1992, stating that the delinquency rate was actually 5.0 percent, and expressing confusion as to how the OCC had arrived at the larger figure. But even the 5.0 percent rate stated by Citi is above the national average.

Because of the 5.0 percent delinquency, Citicorp had been forced by the regulations to repurchase $600 million of previously sold mortgages at the end of the second quarter of 1992.

The Reed Watch. During the latter half of 1991, there was talk—a lot of talk—about the shaky status of Reed. Some observers said he was presiding as CEO on borrowed time, that he would be lucky to last to the end of 1992. Fortunately for him, he has been able to hold on at least for the time being. However, when the unexpected resignation of president Richard Braddock was announced (see Chapter 3), the rumors started up again.

In the long run, perhaps as serious as anything else, is the fact that while Citicorp has been languishing in red ink, other banking companies are in the black and on the move. Consultant David Cates says, "Citicorp is a weakened competitor. It doesn't have resources to compete. It doesn't have capital. It doesn't have liquidity."

At an analyst's meeting last summer, John Reed said that it was quite possible the mergers among large regional banks (see Chapter 12) could mean that Citi would be knocked out of its number-one position. He stated that that would be of little importance by itself; what would be of concern would be if these competitors eroded Citicorp's share of the national consumer banking market. This, of course, is precisely the objective of BankAmerica, NationsBank, Banc One, and others.

For a while, Reed accepted responsibility for the sad state of affairs at Citicorp. That did not stop him from parting company with a number of senior officers, including Lawrence Small (who is now head of Fannie Mae, the Federal National Mortgage Association), Michael Callan, and most recently, Richard Braddock (who recently joined Medco Containment Services, a drug distribution company, as CEO). Well, someone had to take the blame, right? More recently, now that there has been some improvement in the bottom line, the Citicorp CEO seems to want to place the blame elsewhere. One place to do so, quite naturally, is the economy. And while the recession has hurt Citicorp as it has all banking companies, many of the others have made far better progress in getting back in the black.

Still more recently, Reed has blamed some of his problems on the Citicorp culture and the bureaucracy which has built up over the years. But he could have been more forceful in changing the bank's culture.

And only the man at the top can have an impact on the bureaucracy. In fact, it was only when things got seriously bad that Reed appointed a second in command, making the now departed Richard Braddock president. By not doing this earlier, he only perpetuated the combative culture that had been encouraged by Walter Wriston.

During his two-year tenure as president, Braddock was charged with shaping up the operations of the bank and exerting strong control over costs, much like Reed had done 20 years before. From all the evidence available, it had seemed that Braddock was just the person to bring a little discipline to the organization. Now, as the news release announcing his resignation stated, Braddock's "responsibilities will be assumed by other members of the senior corporate management team."

John Reed has been acting more like a manager. But as he has done in the past, he's waited until it is awfully late in the day.

11

All the Wrong Moves

We've already discussed some of Citicorp's mistakes. For a big bank with a lot of high-priced help, it does seem to do more than its share of wrong things from time to time. Maybe it's just an illusion, but it appears that the mistakes are happening with greater frequency these days. At the same time, it should be pointed out that the mistakes under Reed seem less severe (if that is the right word) than those that occurred during the Wriston years.

The more recent deals that have gone wrong, caused problems, or created embarrassing situations are different. There is less flavor of intrigue and of manipulation. No, these recent events can be better characterized by such evaluations as unknowing, imprudent and, on occasion, just plain stupid.

The Quotron Quandary

A case in point is Quotron. John Reed personally pushed through the purchase of Quotron Systems, Inc., in 1986. The deal for the stock quote system had been cooking since the year before at a price of $630 million (there are some reports that the price was actually $680 million). Reed thought that the purchase was a bargain and that the company would eventually prove to be one of the bank's most profitable subsidiaries. As of mid-1992, Quotron has never shown a profit—and the outlook for improvement in the near-term is less than promising.

There were problems right from the start. Significant changes in Quotron's product mix were planned, so a design group to accomplish the task was established and based at Citicorp's headquarters in New York. The trouble was that Quotron itself was based in California. As you might imagine, communications were less than ideal; they didn't improve much even when the design group was split, with part of the group moved to Quotron's California office.

Then there was the competition. All along the way, it has been tough and aggressive and has included such firms as Automated Data Processing, Reuters Holdings, and Telerate, a unit of Dow Jones. Not only have these information suppliers been competing for the space on the desks of stockbrokers, the situation has been compounded by the fact that Wall Street was less than eager to deal with Citicorp, which many of them consider to be a competitor of theirs for the financial services business.

Reed envisioned Quotron as the cornerstone of Citicorp's unit that supplies information services. Reed believed that this was an area that would lead to big business and bigger profits for the bank—and Quotron would be in the forefront. Walter Wriston, in an interview a couple of years after his retirement agreed with Reed's assessment. "It seems to me a terrific idea," he said. "I think the strategy these fellows have devised is terrific."

A Constant Drag

Unfortunately, over the years, the costs to Citicorp of owning Quotron have increased with every passing year. In 1988, Quotron lost $105 million; in 1989, $179 million; and in 1990, $228 million. In 1991, the bank announced it was writing down its Quotron investment by $400 million; this accounted for about half of Citicorp's horrendous third-quarter 1991 loss.

Not only has Quotron been losing money, it has lost ground to competitors because of its antiquated technology (and it doesn't take long for things to become antiquated in these days of technological advances) and its inability to compete with new products. "They sat on the basic quote terminal too long," according to Andrew Delaney, editor of *Trading Systems Technology*.

Over the years, Quotron has lost a number of sizeable retail accounts, including Merrill Lynch, Shearson Lehman Brothers, and Bear Stearns. In 1992, it lost still another of its major accounts, Kidder, Peabody & Company, to perhaps its toughest competitor, ADP. A week later, Quotron lost its Dean Witter account. This reportedly leaves the firm with only one major Wall Street client still in the fold. Moreover, these latest losses have occurred after Quotron teamed up with IBM to provide customers with standard hardware and software, something ADP had done much earlier. That fact alone does not bode well for the Citicorp subsidiary.

Interestingly, in an issue of *Citibank World*, published for Citi employees early in 1992, the Quotron-IBM alliance was announced, trumpeting that the arrangement would offer customers better machines at lower costs. This upbeat article made no mention of the problems Quotron has been trying to overcome, although stories about the problems of Quotron often appear in the business trade press.

For some time, there have been rumors that Quotron is on the block. Midway through 1992, the official line of the bank was that the subsidiary is not for sale. With well over a billion dollars now invested in Quotron, and with its client base eroding, the truth is more likely that Citi has found no willing takers at a reasonable price. But at what point will the bank finally decide that Reed's dream turned out to be a nightmare and that the smart thing to do is cut its losses?

No Point of Sale

At the time of the $400 million write-down, there was another write-down of $30 million of its "point-of-sale" consumer purchase information unit.

Just what is this point-of-sale (POS) unit all about? According to information supplied by Citicorp, the bank's POS information services has been working for several years with supermarket retailers, consumer package-goods manufacturers, and other marketers to develop household target marketing programs, information services, and database marketing applications, This database contains the actual purchase history of over 2.5 million households. Actual household purchase information is captured electronically at the supermarket point of sale. No surveys or self-reporting studies are involved, just accurate information obtained by an identification card when a purchase is made. Once the information is collected and analyzed, it can be used for target marketing purposes. Citicorp POS also has been involved in providing research studies that range from promotion testing to advertising impact studies.

Since mention was made of this "exciting point-of-sale initiative" in the 1989 annual report, there has been little word on what has been happening, except, as noted above, a write-down of $30 million in the third quarter of 1991. Apparently there have been snags in the development of the system; whether it will be made to work or not, whether it will pay off or not, is anybody's guess.

Information Services. This aspect of the bank's financial services mix was originally pushed by Walter Wriston. In Citicorp's 1983 annual report, he said, "Information about money is becoming almost as important as money itself," and predicted that his bank would be a "major participant in the rapidly growing information business." Wriston made a valid point; managing information could well be one of the major banking challenges in the years ahead. John Reed, of course, also endorsed the concept, with such moves as the point-of-sale initiative and the purchase of Quotron.

Somewhere along the line, something went wrong. In its five-point plan to revitalize Citicorp, unveiled in the 1991 annual report, information services was not included, and John Reed has repeatedly said that for the next few years the bank will concentrate on its core businesses. Obviously, information services is no longer the wave of Citicorp's future.

Why, Oh Why, O&Y?

There have been so many good examples of bad real estate loans at Citicorp that it presents a challenge to pick out just one to cover in detail. The loans to Donald Trump have already been described (see Chapter 2). However, the loans made to Olympia & York Developments, Ltd. (O&Y), the huge Canadian real estate developer that is the largest in the world, may have been some of the worst in Citi's history. They also represent an example in which Citicorp rarely took the role of lead bank, instead following along with the other banks because O&Y was supposed to have been in superb financial shape with solid and savvy management.

However it happened, Citicorp got taken to the cleaners. The O&Y bankruptcy has also led to some major managerial changes within Citicorp.

Development of a Giant Developer

From the very beginning, during the 1950s, the family that has run—and owns—Olympia & York, the Reichmann brothers, have played their cards very close to the vest.

The brothers were born in Vienna, where their father had a prosperous poultry business. The family fled the Nazis in 1938, moving to Paris, then to Madrid, to Tangier, and finally to Toronto. They started a tile business, which is still run by the youngest brother, Ralph. Albert, who is the oldest, together with Paul, began to deal in real estate and formed O&Y, with Paul the chief strategist and Albert the adviser.

Over the years, the firm became known for its willingness to take risks while other real estate developers would be pulling in their wings. The growth of the firm was spectacular, although little was known of its financial condition. Owned by the family, the firm provided almost no details. But the name of the firm was on all sorts of projects, first in Canada, and then in the United States. During the 1970s, O&Y bought any number of office towers in New York City at low, low prices. During the real estate slump in the early 1980s, the brothers sunk billions into the construction of the World Financial Center in lower Manhattan.

The Reichmann real estate empire continued to expand through the 1980s. In fact, the money was rolling in so fast that the brothers decided to expand their horizons and began to invest in energy companies, as well.

But as the 1980s began to wind down and the real estate boom began to collapse, the Reichmanns found that their cashflows could not carry $18 billion worth of debt. The sheer size of the problems at Olympia & York dwarfed the Trumps and the Trammel Crows who were also having problems of their own. Over the years, the Reichmanns had borrowed from an ever-increasing number of banks, in Canada, the United States, Europe, and Japan. Moreover, they had found it easy to borrow and still provide a minimum amount of financial data to the lenders. The Reichmanns had built a reputation of taking risks, and yes, making those risks pay off. Their credit ratings were impeccable. It seemed that nothing was wrong.

Unfortunately, that was not true. With real estate values dropping all around the world, and occupancy rates going down, less and less cash was coming in. Behind the scenes, Paul Reichmann began shuttling between his many banks trying to get his loans restructured. But when 1992 came in, he found that time was running out.

In January, a dispute between O&Y and Morgan Stanley made the papers: it concerned the financing of Morgan Stanley's office tower in the troubled Canary Wharf project in London. The dispute went to court, and in May O&Y was ordered to buy back the building for $240 million. A month later, O&Y commercial paper and other debt instruments were downgraded. This had never happened before. It caused consternation among members of the Reichmann family and chills up and down the backs of their many bankers.

In the middle of March, O&Y canceled a planned public offering for its highly touted Canary Wharf complex that was being built on the site of rotting docks along the Thames in London. There had been horrendous cost overruns and a high vacancy rate in the completed units, which had prompted the Reichmanns to ask for tax concessions; the British government said no.

The next day, the Reichmanns said they would redeem the remaining O&Y paper outstanding and sell Exchange Tower in Toronto to raise cash. And a couple of days later, the company announced publicly what it had been trying to do for weeks previously—restructure its billions of debt spread out among over 100 banks. The reality of a worldwide real estate recession had finally caught up with Olympia & York.

Talking With the Bankers

First there were talks between O&Y officers and the Bank of Canada and the Bank of England. These central bankers were concerned that if the real estate developer was not able to get sufficient cash to service its debt, the result could be a panic in the world markets. Shortly after these talks, O&Y began notifying its banks that it needed money. It also said it would provide the banks with more information about its finances than it ever had in the past.

As meetings with the O&Y bankers began, it became apparent that O&Y would use Canary Wharf as its prime bargaining chip, getting the banks to either accept equity in the development or use it as collateral. It's the biggest asset the Reichmanns have, carrying the least amount of debt—but it is only about one-third completed.

The leaders of the negotiations with O&Y were the Royal Bank of Canada and the Canadian Imperial Bank of Canada, both having as much as $800 million in loans to the developer. Another major participant was the non-Canadian bank with the most exposure, Citibank, which had nearly $500 million in O&Y loans. The negotiations, after weeks of talks and meetings held in various locations, failed. The banks and O&Y officials could not reach an accommodation.

Going Bankrupt.   There was only one thing left to do, a step the Reichmanns did not want to take because of fierce family pride and a conviction that if only the banks would help see them over the hump, things would improve. The banks did not want O&Y to take that step either, fearing the effect it might have on world markets. But O&Y was afraid that after missing a $14.1 million payment on its 72-story First Canadian Place headquarters building, the bondholders would seize the building. To protect its Canadian properties from seizure by creditors, O&Y filed for the Canadian equivalency of bankruptcy. The court issued an order under the country's Companies' Creditors Arrangement Act which would keep creditors at bay until October 1992.

There were 29 O&Y companies taking part in the bankruptcy filings. In addition, four of the companies with U.S. holdings also filed in the Federal Bankruptcy Court in New York for protection under Chapter 11 of the United States Bankruptcy Code. Most of the New York properties do not have the bankruptcy protection at present.

As it turned out, the bankruptcy filings really didn't have all that much impact on the markets. The Canadian banks had already been hit by falling stock prices, which, in turn, had dragged down the entire Canadian stock market. Here in the United States, the banks with the most exposure—Citibank, Chemical, and J. P. Morgan—had been anticipating losses and had already absorbed some of them. Citi had written off $100 million of its O&Y loans in each of the first two quarters of 1992.

Analysts speculated that if the bankruptcy had taken place in 1990, the impact would have been far greater in New York. After all, O&Y is the city's largest landlord, owning 23 million square feet of office space.

At its meetings in London with 15 banks prior to the bankruptcy filings, the developer had asked for a moratorium on most of its interest payments and principal on its debts. The banks refused to accept an exchange of debts for an equity position in Canary Wharf. They had decided to play hardball and were in no mood to compromise. Incidentally, Citibank's negotiations have been handled by William Rhodes, who most recently had successfully negotiated the Brazil debt (see Chapter 7). Now, O&Y has breathing room to continue its negotiations without the sword of foreclosure hanging over the meeting table.

The bankruptcy filings, among other things, have given details on the exposure of banks to such off–balance sheet instruments as interest-rate swap contracts. These contracts are agreements between parties to exchange fixed-rate interest payments for floating-rate interest payments. The dollar amount listed is not the amount of interest rate being swapped but the principal amount of the agreement on which the interest is calculated. O&Y is a heavy participant in such devices, believing they do well for the company. Citicorp is listed as having $260 million in swap contracts. However, the bank says it has no record of the transactions.

The Bottom Line.   Citicorp got involved in Olympia & York without much analysis of the loans or knowing enough about the borrower. And, in this case, good money was pumped in after bad. Many banks, of course, were taken in by O&Y, in no small measure to the personal skills of Paul Reichmann. A Canadian banker is quoted in the October 1992 issue of *Vanity Fair*: "He [Reichmann] presented himself as a humble, reliable visionary, and bank presidents and chairmen just ate it up."

Because the Reichmanns played their trump cards (the bankruptcy filings) with minimal impact on the financial markets, it can be assumed that the banks, including Citicorp, will now be able to set the tone of future negotiations. If this proves to be the case, the banks, again including Citicorp, may not lose too much more than they already have. The wild card in this, of course, is Paul Reichmann; he can be unpredictable.

The O&Y debacle did have one interesting side effect on Citicorp and the way it is run. The president of Citibank Canada, Limited, who was principally responsible for extending credit to the real estate developer, has left after 23 years with the company. Officially, he resigned to "pursue other interests."

Another Real Estate–Related Mistake

The Olympia & York experience has demonstrated that the real estate market in London has fared just as poorly as real estate in New York and in most other parts of the United States. Another London real estate loan has resulted in a $120 million loss to Citicorp. This happened during the spring of 1992 when Citi placed Randsworth PLC in receivership, which is the British equivalent of a forced filing of bankruptcy.

The Citicorp action also meant that JMB Realty of Chicago and its pension fund clients lost their entire $424 million investment in Randsworth, a real estate company with properties concentrated in London's West End.

For JMB, this was a most embarrassing situation. One of the largest real estate investors in the United States, it has about $26 billion under its management. JMB president Neil Bluhm is reported to have said, "It was the worst investment we ever made."

The investment was not much better for Citicorp. At its best level, the JMB investors had valued the Randsworth investment around $444 million. Citicorp's exposure was $335 million. There is approximately $229 million in a subsidiary of Randsworth, but those holders have a claim senior to Citicorp's, which leaves the bank with a $120 million loss.

The receivership action forced by Citicorp was no surprise, since the Randsworth investment had turned sour in 1990. At that time, JMB asked its investors, which included the pension funds of Illinois, Massachusetts, and Oregon, to ante up £130 million more to help finance the takeover of Randsworth. The pension fund investors, reading the handwriting on the wall, have, for the most part, already written down their investments. Actually, Citicorp probably has done the same thing; John Reed said at one point that the bank had cleaned up its real estate portfolio in London during the fourth quarter of 1991, which meant that Citicorp had written down its Randsworth investment.

While Randsworth struggled with its properties, JMB wrangled with Citicorp over a restructuring of the debt. When nothing could be worked out, Citi took the receivership action. Foreclosures in the United

States can take years to work their way through the courts. That isn't the case in Great Britain, where receiverships are settled quickly. However, about all Citicorp can do with the Randsworth retail and office properties in the depressed London real estate market is hold on to them and pray for a turnaround—soon.

Another Way to Lose.   Banking companies can lose on real estate by lending directly to an individual who has a good track record and a sales persona (Donald Trump), or to a real estate developer with a AAA rating (Olympia & York), or to a firm that has usually invested wisely and well (JMB Realty). Unfortunately, Citicorp has done all of these any number of times.

Another way to lose is by buying second mortgages from the originators of the loans. This is how most of the second-mortgage lenders get their capital, by selling the mortgage paper to large banks such as Citibank. Fully 10 percent of all second mortgages are pooled for the secondary market. The problem is that some bad loans get into the pool.

The Dartmouth Plan, a second-mortgage lender based in New York City, bought many of the loans originated by Dartmouth during a good part of the 1980s. Then, in 1985, Dartmouth paid $3 million to settle a suit which charged that it had been involved in misleading lending practices. The suit had been filed by the attorney general of the state of Connecticut. In paying the $3 million, Dartmouth did not admit or deny that it had done anything wrong.

Citibank—and this is where the bank should have known better—kept on buying the Dartmouth second mortgages until it stopped doing so in 1989. At that point, according to Citibank, there were clear problems with lending practices of the second-mortgage lender. Dartmouth claimed it had never made a fraudulent loan, but the firm went out of business in early 1990; none of the big banks would buy its mortgage paper.

More Mistakes

Mistakes will happen in any organization; the bigger the organization, the more mistakes will be made—and chances are that some of those mistakes will be whoppers. Not only that, when mistakes are made at large and important organizations, there's a better chance that what happened will make the papers. And when the organization is not universally adored, those items in the papers are apt to be prominently displayed.

This is certainly true with Citicorp, a financial giant that many love to hate. Here are just a few mistakes that have happened in recent years.

How Not to Handle
Canceled Bonds

Between 1974 and 1986, Citicorp accumulated canceled corporate securities for safekeeping and later destruction when they were no longer needed. The face value of these securities amounted to approximately $111 billion, and, according to the Office of the Comptroller of the Currency, filled some 3500 boxes.

Then some of these supposedly destroyed securities appeared in various parts of the world. They were fraudulently presented for transfer or even used as collateral for loans, and there was nothing to indicate that they were other than legitimate.

Many banks do this, acting as agents for corporations and maintaining necessary records for securities that had matured or had been redeemed. When the stocks and bonds are canceled, the standard procedure followed by Citicorp and others is to perforate the paper so that there is no question of the status of the securities. These boxes of worthless securities were supposedly sent by the bank to an outside firm, MSM, which would get rid of them during 1985 and 1986. Since 1987, Citicorp has handled the destruction of canceled certificates.

It seems, however, that not all of the paper was, in fact, perforated. Some of these canceled securities were circulated in Europe as early as 1987.

Late in the fall of 1991, in the United States the Comptroller of the Currency and the Securities and Exchange Commission, together with law enforcement officials, began to investigate a worldwide scheme involving the sale of these securities. The paper of some top firms were included in the scheme—ARCO, Boeing, McDonald's, even Citicorp itself. The worthless securities were eventually traced back to the bank and those boxes of worthless stocks and bonds that had been transferred to MSM in Staten Island for destruction. At the time, Citicorp decided to destroy the old certificates itself; according to the Comptroller's office, "MSM's document destruction consisted of a vacant lot with an empty trailer."

The Comptroller of the Currency accused Citicorp of willfully violating securities laws by not making sure the canceled stocks and bonds were safe. It also charged that the bank had not properly notified the authorities of the possible misuse of securities under its control.

Without admitting or denying guilt in the matter, Citicorp settled the charges by the bank regulator in June 1992. It agreed to take measures to ensure that similar incidents would not be repeated. In a statement issued at the time of the settlement, Citi stated that it had fully cooperated with such government agencies as the Federal Bureau of Investigation, the Drug Enforcement Administration, and Interpol during the investigation.

Actually, the bank had joined with the Comptroller's office earlier in the year in issuing warnings about the possible misuse of the securities.

Unfortunately, the warning came too late for some dealers who had already been stung by the scam.

One of those dealers, it seems, was Smith Barney, Harris Upham & Company, which has sued Citibank, the Citicorp unit involved in all of this, claiming that Smith Barney was a victim in efforts to use the worthless securities. Smith Barney said it had arranged to buy $6.3 million in Dow Chemical bonds from a government-controlled bank in Liechtenstein, only to find out a few days later that Citibank had canceled the bonds over a decade ago. To make matters worse, before it learned the true status of the bonds, it had sold them almost immediately to a third party. This meant Smith Barney had to buy additional Dow securities to cover the contract. Citi says it has no liability and no material financial exposure in the matter. It is understood that the suit is still pending. Citicorp has stated that the lawsuit is "without merit."

Lack of Control

Citicorp has long been known for its decentralized operations, which Walter Wriston long championed. While decentralization provides an organization with many advantages, there is a downside, as well, and that is lack of control. John Reed apparently is moving toward more centralization, which would, of course, allow headquarters to exercise the kind of control that seems to have been lacking at Citicorp Establishment Services (CES), which was sold in June 1992 (see Chapter 1).

CES, the third largest credit card processing operation in the country, processed nearly $30 billion in card transactions in 1990 for 97,000 clients, according to *The Nilson Report*, which covers the credit card industry. However, because the processing business is so competitive and profit margins are relatively thin, the unit was an obvious asset for Citicorp to sell. Of perhaps more immediate concern to the parent company was the fact that the top management of the unit had been caught overstating revenues and had been fired.

Approximately $23 million in revenue had been inflated over a two-year period. This went on for so long, without detection, apparently because the unit's financial officers were involved. The bank was forced to restate its revenue by that amount in the third quarter of 1991 to reflect the error. The former president of the unit and 11 senior and middle-level executives were dismissed.

Why did these CES officers inflate revenue? Bank officials gave no reason, but they did confirm that any bonuses received by the employees were directly tied to the performance of the unit.

The India Stock Market Scandal

Citicorp has had a presence in India since 1902. During the past decade, it has been in the forefront of bringing consumer banking to the country. As a result, the Citibank unit in India has seen profits soar, from $11.4 million in 1990 to over $49 million in 1992.

Unfortunately, Citi has been named in a developing financial scandal involving major Indian and foreign banks, finance companies, and brokers who are alleged to have diverted both bank and corporate funds into the stock market. According to government reports, many banks violated federal laws while trading in government bonds and investing money for corporate clients.

While all the details are not known, the cost of the scandal reached $1.25 billion at the end of 1992; the Bombay stock exchange crashed in April of 1992, falling 800 points in a week; at least 25 people have been arrested, and thousands of people have been left bankrupt.

Just what role, if any, Citibank has played in all of this is still not known. But Citi's officer in charge of the Bombay-based international banking and finance group has been transferred to New York. In addition, the Reserve Bank of India declined to extend the appointment of the senior vice president and country manager for India of Bank of America. The chief officers in India of the two British banks named in the scandal, ANZ Grindlay's Bank and Standard Chartered Bank, have been replaced.

According to the Associated Press, India has sent three official reports to the U.S. Securities and Exchange Commission, at the SEC's request.

Where all of this will lead is anyone's guess. But it is the kind of trouble Citicorp does not need as it struggles to get back on the right track.

Better Management—and Better Management Policies

Rules can be tightened, controls can be strengthened, procedures can be written. And after all of this, mistakes will continue to happen. At least the possibility for mistakes will be minimized. It does look as if John Reed and his management team are beginning to take the kind of steps that will minimize the commitment of mistakes...finally.

In no area of a bank are these procedures more important than in the extension of credit. Bad loans have swamped Citicorp during the 1990s, resulting in the kind of losses that seem to have overwhelmed John Reed and the rest of the organization's management team. At last, there are changes being made. Reed told a meeting of analysts in June 1992 that a new credit process would be presented to the Citicorp board of directors. Just what is included was not spelled out, but he did mention that his people would be spending a great deal of time worrying about the "externalities" in the lending process. This procedure is something new for Citicorp, because it means that the entire picture of a borrower must be taken into account.

These developments bring to mind a statement made by Walter Wriston almost 20 years ago, one that may be most appropriate to the current situation:

> We have a rule around the Citibank that balance sheets don't pay back loans, only people do. It probably is the most basic thing in the extension of credit. Banks that are managed by people of character who know what they are doing will succeed. If you have bum management in banks, there's nothing that's going to save them.

What can be added to that statement? It says it all.

12

Losing the
Competitive Edge

Back in the 1970s and 1980s, Citicorp was on the cutting edge of banking innovation. As an organization, it developed new ideas, encouraged experimentation, put fresh concepts into place, and successfully moved the entire industry forward. If there was any one banking company that could be considered the leader in the field of financial services, it was Citicorp. In fact, during the mid-1980s, it was more than the leader; Citicorp was head and shoulders above the rest. No matter what moves the competition made, Citicorp was able to stay in front of them and, more often than not, increase its lead.

More recently, it has lost that edge, it has lost its leadership position—and its leadership role—in the banking industry. And there is a good chance it could lose its place as the largest bank in the country.

During the past three years or so, while Citicorp under the management of John Reed has been licking its wounds and working hard at damage control, the competition the corporation faces has been changing, getting stronger, increasing in size, becoming more innovative, solidifying their franchises, and adding new players. These changes do not bode well for this bank that once was the greatest of them all.

As noted elsewhere, the economic downturn in the 1990s has hurt Citicorp. But it has also hurt to one degree or another all the competitive banks in Citi's financial marketplace. The catch is that many of the other banking companies with which Citicorp must compete have been able to recover faster or have taken steps permitting them to post at least reasonably good performance figures, thereby growing and prospering while Citi has done little more than mark time. Although Citicorp did show a profit for the first three quarters of 1992 (and probably for the entire year), the local competition such as Chemical Bank has actually earned more money. The net result of all this is that Citi, if anything, has been losing ground.

The question that is before us now is, Why hasn't Citicorp been able to do the same kind of thing? Why has its recovery been so sluggish? What's holding Citi back?

What's a Bank To Do?   There are any number of things banks and their holding companies can do to grow and become stronger: cut expenses, clean out bad loans and raise lending standards, increase capital through equity sales and retained earnings (assuming there are any earnings to retain). Citicorp is doing all these things, except for that latter item. Other banks are also cutting costs and upgrading their loan portfolios. And many of those banks are reporting substantial gains in earnings. After a comparison of what Citicorp has done and what several of its competitor banks have done, the best that can be said for Citi is that it has kept pace; the worst that can be said is that the competition is gaining.

However, the quickest, and currently most popular, way for a bank to grow is through mergers and acquisitions. These days, it seems that every bank holding company but Citicorp is going the merger route—and some of the mergers that have taken place recently have been spectacular.

Mergers and Acquisitions

Looking only at the domestic retail banking segment of its business, Citicorp has slowed its growth through acquisition to absolutely zero. During the seven complete calendar years under John Reed's command, this is what has been happening:

1985

- Agreed to acquire the Great Western Bank & Trust in Arizona, adding 36 new branch offices
- Received full banking privileges in Maryland
- Bought a savings and loan in Nevada

1986

- Opened doors to full-service banking in Maryland, Arizona, the District of Columbia, Nevada, and Utah
- Completed the acquisition of Great Western

- Opened Citibank Maryland
- Bought National Permanent, a 14-branch thrift in the District of Columbia

1987

- Added branches in Utah, California, and Maryland

1988

- Bought the credit card business of First Republic Bank, Dallas, adding 700,000 new cardholders
- Acquired the United Bank of Arizona, increasing Citi's total branches in Arizona to 60
- Bought Caribank in south Florida with 14 branches

1989

- No significant acquisitions

1990

- No significant acquisitions

1991

- No significant acquisitions

Interestingly, this situation was mentioned (somewhat obliquely) in the Citicorp 1989 annual report with the following statement:

> We recognize we are competing in a fast-changing marketplace, buffeted by S&L crises, a seemingly chronic overcapacity in the industry, an inadequate, regulatory apparatus, and other economic uncertainties. While these factors contribute to instability, they should also offer us opportunities to extend our geographic reach and product breadth in the coming years—especially as the inefficient players weed themselves out. The combination we are putting in place—integrated product sets, national capacity, and an uncompromising customer service culture—should serve us well in this respect.

These are excellent words, but what do they mean? They mean that plenty of blame is to be spread around for the lack of forward progress but that none of that touches anyone at the bank. And following the publication of these stirring words, as noted, there has been an extended period in which essentially no growth through acquisition or merger has occurred.

Of course, part of the problem is that Citicorp has had precious little money to spare these days for acquisitions or for much of anything else. Then, particularly with its capital position not meeting the regulatory standards, new or old, during the three years in question, there was no guarantee that approval by the bank regulators would be forthcoming.

This particular situation was specifically addressed in the prospectus for the recent issue of preferred stock. Citicorp states that the company had signed a memorandum of understanding with the Federal Reserve and the comptroller's office agreeing to secure their approval before becoming engaged in an acquisition (see Chapter 1).

Meanwhile, Across the Street

At a meeting of the New York Bankers Association in January, 1991, the president of the Federal Reserve Bank of New York, E. Gerald Corrigan, signaled the support of the regulators for mergers between large banks. This development is something that has not always been encouraged by bank administrators. Corrigan also stressed how imperative it was for banks to have adequate capital, a point he had made in no uncertain terms a couple of months earlier in a meeting with John Reed the previous fall (see Chapter 1).

After noting the potential cost savings and other economies of scale that could be gained by teaming up, Corrigan commented to the members of the Association, "I would be very surprised—perhaps disappointed—if when we meet here next year, one or more mergers among the largest banks in the United States are not already a reality."

Apparently not wishing to disappoint Corrigan, there have been a number of remarkable mergers during 1991 and 1992, with several of them breaking records in the size of the institutions joining forces. The three singled out below have now become the three largest banks in the country next to Citicorp. Their equity capital as a percentage of assets all surpasses Citicorp's capital, as do their reserves as a proportion of nonperforming loans. Two (BankAmerica and NationsBank) have more branches than Citi, and one (BankAmerica) has a greater number of ATMs. All of this spells big trouble with a capital T for Citicorp as the banks begin to compete in the financial marketplace.

BankAmerica/Security Pacific

Enjoying reasonably good financial health again, and now headed by a bank marketing dynamo whose ambitions seem to know no bounds,

BankAmerica Corporation in San Francisco announced during the summer of 1991 plans to acquire its largest California rival, cash-short and bad-loan-long Security Pacific Corporation, based in Los Angeles.

Over the past few years, BankAmerica has come roaring back from the brink of collapse, first under the direction of former CEO Tom Clausen, who had done much to put the bank in harm's way in the first place but who had returned to help get things back on track. Now under the leadership of Richard Rosenberg, BankAmerica apparently has been able to put it all together, and perhaps there are some lessons to be learned by Citicorp in what had been done (see Chapter 13).

A done deal as of April 22, 1992, the new banking company presently has assets of about $189 billion, just $27 billion less than Citicorp. It has $13.5 billion in equity capital, which is nearly 40 percent *more* than Citi. It is doing business in 11 western states, and holds more deposits in California, Nevada, and Washington than any other bank. BankAmerica actually has full-service banking operations in 10 of the 11 states (the other state is Hawaii). That means it is one up on Citicorp, which has been trying to blanket the country with full-service banking offices for decades. Citi currently has full-service banking in eight states and the District of Columbia.

This development also means that now Citicorp will be facing a strong—and eager—competitor for a nationwide franchise, should it decide to continue on that route. BankAmerica officials indicate that they are definitely interested in spanning the country, perhaps joining up with a rich and healthy east coast bank. Being realistic about the situation, that event is not likely to happen until the regulators are more comfortable with the idea, which might take a few years, but you never know. BankAmerica CEO Richard Rosenberg will only say, somewhat enigmatically, that "our objective is to build on the strengths of both institutions."

Not that making this megamerger work will be all that easy. Even though BankAmerica has come back a long way, it still has a sizeable block of troubled loans on its books. Of course, they are not even close to the numbers of such loans at Security Pacific (or at Citicorp, for that matter). BankAmerica did have Security Pacific write off many of the worst loans during the nine months the merger was being processed, which helps. In addition, the smaller bank has other strengths, including at least $1.5 billion in goodwill and a deep reservoir of managerial talent.

Moreover, there is a great deal of room for cost cutting, of people and of places. A number of the branches of the combined banks now are redundant, and closing them could result in substantial cost savings. It will take time to fully realize the potential of the two institutions, perhaps as many as three years. However, many of the plans have been in place for quite a while and BankAmerica management began to act upon them even before the merger papers were signed. Both institutions have strong managerial resources, and they will be invaluable and necessary as the organization begins to spread its wings eastward.

Those plans may already be paying off. During the second quarter of 1992, earnings for the combined banks fell by 12 percent, but it should be remembered that Security Pacific was losing money all of 1991. In the third quarter of 1992, BankAmerica's profits rebounded with a solid performance. Loan loss charges were less and cost savings were greater than projected by most analysts. In addition, BankAmerica now has reserves amounting to 98 percent of its nonaccruing assets; this is about double the average of reserves at the nation's top 25 banks. All of this good news prompted bank stock analyst Thomas Hanley of First Boston Corporation to comment, "This is an outstanding quarter, and this is one hell of a management team."

As an aside to this, during Rosenberg's first 15 months as BankAmerica chief executive, before announcement of the Security Pacific merger in the summer of 1991, his bank acquired $14.5 billion worth of assets in six western states. Most of these were parts of insolvent thrifts—the better parts, it is safe to assume. He also tried to take over part of the Bank of New England, in order to gain a foothold on the east coast. However, the Federal Reserve did not approve the deal. But the effort does show that BankAmerica and Richard Rosenberg are wasting no time in making tracks along the roads across America.

Chemical Bank/Manufacturers Hanover Trust

Both Chemical Bank and Manufacturers Hanover Trust had been struggling for years, even before the recession hit. Yet the marriage of the two would appear to be a natural; it even may be a case where the whole will be more than the sum of its parts. The second-quarter 1992 earnings of the combined bank increased to $240 million, bringing the total earnings for the first half of the year to half a billion dollars. Not only that, third-quarter 1992 earnings were above expectations, with a 20 percent increase. Part of this performance is due to the fact that cost savings originally contemplated by joining the two banks together are already more than expected. When the combined banking company lops off 70 or more branches in 1992 and 1993, the costs savings will mount even more.

Consummated at the beginning of 1992, the merger was supposedly a marriage of equals. But the name is now Chemical Banking Corporation. John McGillicuddy, who was CEO of Manufacturers Hanover before the merger, is the present CEO of Chemical; in 1994, Walter Shipley, who had been CEO of the old Chemical Bank, will succeed McGillicuddy as CEO of the new bank. The Chemical side probably has the best reserve of management talent; for at least a decade, rumors dogged Manufacturers Hanover about its imminent demise and, in fact, at one point it had been a serious candidate for a forced takeover. Many of the good people at Manufacturers Hanover decided not to wait for the ultimate to happen which, of course, did the bank no good at all.

The major point about this particular merger is that Chemical is now the third largest bank in the country—and it has 600 or so offices right in Citicorp's front (or back) yard. With approximately $135 billion in assets, it has jumped far ahead of Chase Manhattan (which used to be second to Citi in New York with $98 billion in assets). Moreover, the combined Chemical–Manufacturers Hanover consumer accounts total 1.2 million households in the New York market; Citicorp has about 1.6 million consumer accounts. With its added resources, Chemical is expected to give Citicorp a real run for the local consumer business. As Allan DeCotiis, the head of PSI, a bank consulting firm based in Tampa, says, this will "lead to head-to-head competitive banking between Chemical and Citibank like you have never seen before."

Although it has a long distance to go, Chemical is getting closer to the big one, and at last the organization has the resources, financial and otherwise, which are necessary for it to compete effectively with any bank, regardless of size. Moreover, the new bank apparently has decided to go in the direction of its strengths, which primarily lie in the consumer banking area. This was signaled early on by Shipley, who stated that "the lemming era of banking is over."

NationsBank

The *ménage à trois* between NCNB (North Carolina), Sovran Bank (Virginia), and Citizens & Southern (Georgia) has created the fourth largest bank holding company in the country, with nearly $120 billion in assets. The fact that none of the banks involved are in money centers indicates just how far the regionals have come since regional banking across neighboring state borders was permitted.

Under the aggressive, abrasive, innovative, and apparently quite persuasive leadership of Hugh McColl, NCNB had shown every indication of wanting to become more than a superregional banking company. He had already moved into Texas and several southeastern states before NationsBank was formed. And the name chosen for the new bank, of course, says everything.

The move into Texas, in 1988 with the acquisition of what was left of First RepublicBank Corporation, was instructive of the willingness of Hugh McColl to tread where few other angels would get their big toes wet. Congress complained, and there was outright hostility on the part of some Texans. Yet NCNB made almost all of its 1990 earnings from the Texas operation, which helped provide the strength to establish NationsBank.

McColl's latest move is an agreement to invest some $200 million in MNC Financial, Inc., based in Baltimore. MNC has had a lot of real estate loan troubles but seems to be working itself out of that deep hole. If this recovery continues, NationsBank will be in a good position to acquire the Maryland bank; if the recovery sputters, its exposure will not be all that much. And if NationsBank does acquire MNC, it will be the deposit leader in the Washington-Maryland-Virginia area. This is what Citicorp had hoped to be when it moved into the District of Columbia and Maryland in the mid-1980s (see Chapter 9).

Other Mergers

There are plenty of other bank consolidations taking place all around the country. As Edward Annunziato of Merrill Lynch & Company observed, "The race is on for market share." Citicorp, however, at this point in time, is not even entered in the race.

Among those institutions already running, and running rather strongly, are:

- Banc One, based in Columbus, Ohio. It has strung together a chain of banks in several states, mostly in the midwest. Already this year, CEO John McCoy has bought Valley National Bank, the largest and last independent bank in Arizona, as well as Key Centurian Bancshares, the largest bank in West Virginia.

- Barnett Banks and First Florida Banks have linked up, leaving only one independent left in the state of Florida.

- KeyCorp, which is based in the northeast, has acquired Puget Sound Bancorp in Washington.

- Norwest Corporation, Richard Kovachevich's bank headquartered in Minneapolis, bought United Banks of Colorado last year, to add to its position in several northern middle west states.

There are plenty of other examples. Wells Fargo, the third largest bank in California, was interested in acquiring Security Pacific before BankAmerica finally moved in. Carl Reichardt, CEO of Wells Fargo, had backed off because of the bad loans (and right now he has enough of his own). But he is looking at the possibility of joining forces with First Interstate, which has units in several western states. Incidentally, a few years ago when BankAmerica was in trouble, First Interstate tried to buy it.

What all this means, of course, is that much of the expansion territory is being gobbled up. There are a few attractive franchises left—one possibility is First Chicago, the parent of the First National Bank of Chicago. There seem to be several potential suitors waiting in line. But not Citicorp. Apparently it isn't even looking around at present, in hopes of a brighter tomorrow. The retail banking market in the United States could become fully banked, or at least all the big banks would be spoken for, by the time Citicorp is ready and able to join the merger parade.

In one of the more recent developments on the competitive front, four powerful regional banks—Banc One; CoreStates Financial, Philadelphia; PNC Financial Corporation, Pittsburgh; and Society Corporation, Cleveland—announced that they are teaming up to consolidate electronic banking operations and to process debit transactions. This alliance, stretching from the midwest to the Atlantic seaboard, is expected to offer considerable economies of scale and to strengthen the banks' base in the marketplaces they serve. It is expected that this move will result in the consolidation of ATMs into a single system and a unification of the banks' point-of-sale network. The four regionals also expect to pool their research efforts in the development of new products and services.

When asked about the bank merger mania sweeping the country, John Reed said that Citicorp had no plans to join in the feeding frenzy for the time being. He noted that he is concentrating on working to cut costs and increase capital. These things, he added, "will turn out to be far more productive...[leaving his bank] in a stronger position vis-à-vis the merged banks."

Cost cutting and raising capital are absolutely essential for Citicorp. But that last statement sounds more like wishful thinking than a cold assessment of the situation.

In many ways McColl, and perhaps BankAmerica's Richard Rosenberg, as well, are examples of the kind of rough, tough, savvy, and imaginative banking executives that used to be routinely found in leadership positions at the New York City banks. Add to those two the smoother but just as savvy John McCoy of Banc One, and you see that John Reed and Citicorp are facing strong competition all across the country.

National Branches. Along with the urge to merge, there is an ongoing effort on the part of the regional banks to push Congress to permit true nationwide branching. When this segment was part of last year's unsuccessful bank reform bill, it drew the vociferous opposition of insurance agents because the measure would have allowed banks to, among other things, sell insurance.

Now six regional banks, led by NationsBank under Hugh McColl, are trying to work a deal with the Independent Insurance Agents of America to support interstate banking if the banks agree to place limits on the amount of insurance they write.

Small banks, as might be expected, strongly oppose the plan to let the big banks into even more states than they are in right now. But even some of the big banks are against the compromise. Citicorp, which already sells insurance through a Delaware subsidiary, really doesn't want any more competition.

Competition From Other Directions

Fidelity Investments, in Boston, is the largest seller of mutual funds in the country, with $172 billion under its management. Now it wants to move into the financial service business, selling other products, including credit cards and insurance.

If Fidelity's plan works, it would put the company in direct competition with such firms as Prudential, Merrill Lynch—and Citicorp. At this point, can Citi cope with the added competition, particularly one that is marketing oriented and profitable?

Last year, Fidelity had record revenues totaling $1.5 billion, an increase of 16 percent over the previous year. Its profits were $90 million, a remarkable 182 percent increase. Moreover, since the company is privately held, the financial figures released probably are, if anything, understated.

Fidelity Chairman Edward C. Johnson believes the key to future growth for his company is to redefine the company's relationships with its customers. By directly marketing new financial services and products to its present customers, the company will be in head-to-head competition with brokers and banks, including Citicorp.

What is important here is that such competition is coming from directions an organization such as Citicorp has not planned upon. There could be others waiting to see if Fidelity is successful; if it is, watch out.

Overseas, Too. Citicorp has had a powerful presence overseas, and it plans to remain an active player internationally (not like BankAmerica, which apparently has decided to focus its considerable resources on the United States). But other banks are not going to take the Citicorp challenge lying down.

In many countries, Citicorp has almost had free rein on consumer banking. Now there are signs that such powerful banks as Deutsche Bank and others want some of this business and are planning to go after it. And in Switzerland, the Swiss banks, which have more or less been sleeping in such areas as stock trading, money management, and trade finance, are showing signs of waking up. This means that competition is opening up on still another front for beleaguered Citicorp.

Can the Edge Be Resharpened?

Of course the edge can be resharpened if the bank is willing to take the time and absorb the costs (human and otherwise), and if it really wants to.

But first, Citicorp must recoup its losses. It must get out from under those suffocating real estate loans that promise to be a drag on earnings for years (see Chapter 11). This task is not going to be easy, and John Reed has admitted as much. He said that second-half loan losses will remain high, although less than in the first half of 1992, and that real estate losses appear to have reached a plateau. Taking into account the earnings reported for the first three quarters of 1992 and the less-than-spectacular earnings for the full year, Citicorp must hope its loan portfolio improves a great deal and fast. Its earnings currently amount to 31 cents for every $100 of assets. This compares with Chemical's 70 cents and Banc One's $1.52.

Citicorp also must set (or reset) its priorities and regain its confidence. Since 1987, when Reed led his bank and much of the rest of the industry in facing up to the troubled loans to developing countries, Citicorp has hardly acted like the leader of the banking industry. For that matter, except for that one instance, John Reed has never performed like the spokesperson for the industry, a role that Walter Wriston reveled in.

In other words, Citicorp, over time, may well be able to regain its competitive edge. But it is not all that certain that it will have the resources—and just as importantly, the will—to do so.

13

Learning From BankAmerica

As discussed rather pointedly in the preceding chapter, one of Citicorp's major competitors is now BankAmerica, a bank for which obituaries had been written just a few short years ago. Yet this California giant has come back from the dead and is now bigger and probably better than ever before.

How was BankAmerica able to turn itself around? Its problems were not the same as Citicorp's problems, although there were some similarities. Are there lessons to be learned from the Bank of America experience? And if so, would Reed and his group even be willing to listen?

BankAmerica at the Brink

During the late 1970s, BankAmerica was still the largest banking company in the country. But Citicorp, under the hell-bent-for-leather leadership of Walter Wriston, was coming on strong.

Of course, BankAmerica was also led at the time by a strong-minded leader, who was also autocratic in both manner and deed, Alden Winship (Tom) Clausen. And Clausen was unhappy about the possibility of losing out to Citicorp—to Wriston, in particular—in terms of performance.

Clausen was almost obsessed with the bottom line. His bank had to show a profit, no matter what the cost. During his tenure, BankAmerica reported profits in every year. To accomplish this, other things that should have been done were not. Shortcuts were sometimes taken; reserves that should have been set aside were not. Clausen was concerned that the bottom line was in the black. For some years, that concern was of little consequence; the business of the bank was growing, deposits were increasing, assets were building.

In the long run, however, the bank was hurt by this obsession that profits must be reported. In some instances, it was placed at a distinct disadvantage.

Nowhere was this disadvantage more pronounced than with the bank's investment in technology. Although it had been the first bank in the United States, if not the world, to use computers, it did not place necessary funds in the technology that would speed up record keeping and improve back-office processing. Quite simply, under Clausen, BankAmerica was not investing for the future; instead, it was deliberately extracting more and more profits out of the operations.

In doing all of this, the bank continued to rely on an extensive and expensive branch system throughout the state of California instead of modernizing the delivery of services to customers.

It refused to go the ATM route. Bank studies indicated that ATMs simply would never pay for themselves. While other banks, most notably Citicorp, were building their ATM base (although they dealt with such consequences as high costs and little or no profits), BankAmerica just stayed out of the loop.

In his almost obsessive efforts to cut costs, Clausen sometimes emulated President Jimmy Carter by becoming enmeshed with details and oftentimes neglecting the big picture. For example, he personally had to approve salary increases for anyone in the organization earning $20,000 or more. This was a way to exert control in a decentralized organization, but real control eluded him. And, even with this kind of attention to detail, expenses continued to increase.

As a result, Clausen was sowing the seeds of trouble for the bank at some point down the line. In retrospect, the Clausen years could be described as years of not only mismanagement, but misdirected management. Before the troubles came to the fore, however, Tom Clausen grew tired of the BankAmerica routine and looked for a new challenge. Late in 1980, he announced that he was stepping down as chairman of BankAmerica to become chief of the World Bank.

Before taking his leave, however, Clausen wanted to maintain his 10-year record of ever-increasing profits. However, conditions were working against him, and his record was in jeopardy. Samuel Armacost, who was head cashier of the bank (a position rare in banking these days), was in a position to turn the tide, and that's what he did. Among the steps he took in the fourth quarter of 1980 was to send a memo to each division to either increase profits by 5 percent or lower expenses by 5 percent. He also took the controversial step of changing the value of BankAmerica's investments in a number of venture capital companies. Instead of valuing this portfolio as he had in the past, carrying the investments at their original cost, he priced them at their current market value.

These steps boosted the bottom line and allowed profits to increase over the previous year. Clausen was happy, the stockholders were happy, and Armacost assured himself of getting the top spot at the bank when Clausen left.

Armacost's Legacy

Almost everyone, both inside and outside the bank, hailed the election of Samuel Armacost as president and chief executive officer, to become effective April 1, 1981. At the time, no one saw the irony of installing the new CEO on April Fool's day. Certainly the great majority of BankAmerica employees welcomed Armacost, who promised to be a radical change from the austere and demanding Clausen.

Unfortunately for Armacost and for the bank, the troubles Clausen had sown began to manifest themselves during the new president's first year. First-quarter 1981 profits fell by 19 percent over the year-earlier figure—the first drop in profits in 14 years. Although Armacost had just taken over, he had the responsibility of making the announcement.

Everyone, including the recently departed Tom Clausen, knew that the bank's troubles were just beginning. The investments that had been made in recent years were not in those areas in which profits were strongest or the growth potential was greatest. Its real estate loan portfolio was in poor shape, and its foreign loan business was even worse. Management was perhaps as thin as at any major bank in the country. This was a time for decisive action, for strong leadership at the top.

That needed leadership was not forthcoming. As a result, over the next few years, BankAmerica's condition deteriorated, and profits began to fall, going from a profit of $646 million in 1980 to a loss of $337 million in 1985.

Armacost, however, did make some gutsy, even brilliant moves. In November of 1981, for example, he acquired the premier discount brokerage firm of Charles Schwab & Company. In 1983, BankAmerica acquired the troubled but strategically placed Seafirst Corporation in Seattle. The only problem was that these two additions did not correct BankAmerica's underlying problems; in fact, for the near term, they only worsened the situation.

At the same time, Armacost was proving to be an ineffective manager, disputes between officials mounted, and no real management team was being built.

The losses continued to mount, although Armacost had taken some steps to stem the hemorrhaging, such as selling assets, including its headquarters building in San Francisco. But nothing stemmed the flow. During 1986, as the losses built (the loss for the year amounted to $519 million), there was growing dissension on the board. Charles Schwab resigned. The bank was losing deposits, and its ratings by almost everyone were going down. And to add insult to injury, First Interstate

Bank, an institution far smaller than BankAmerica, made an offer to take over the larger institution. The man behind the offer was Joseph Pinola, who had worked for Tom Clausen in the 1970s.

Finally, in October 1986, the board decided that it had to act. Rumors of Armacost's dismissal had been swirling around for weeks before the actual event occurred. But who was to replace him? The board examined any number of possibilities, but the people they were considering were all found to be unsuited for the job at hand. Surprisingly—to employees, to stockholders, to the banking and investment community, and probably to most of the customers, the board asked Tom Clausen to come back.

How could the board have even considered such a move? Didn't they realize that Clausen was the architect of many of the things that had brought BankAmerica to the position in which it found itself? The board did, in fact, realize this. But they also felt more comfortable with a Clausen in charge instead of an outsider. And they felt that there was no one else on board who could handle the challenge. Moreover, without accepting all the blame, Clausen had publicly stated that he had been overly concerned with the short term during his earlier tenure. Besides, having been passed over for another term as president of the World Bank, he had let his friends know he was ready and eager to come back.

Clausen Again

The press was hardly sanguine about the return of A. W. Clausen. And they had some telling points. During the spring of 1987, when John Reed forced the banking industry to deal more realistically with its Latin American loans, Clausen was hesitant to go along, claiming there were more pressing problems to deal with. Eventually, he agreed to set aside $1.1 billion against those loans, a far smaller percentage for a very sizeable portfolio than what most of the other banks were doing.

In its October 7, 1987, issue, *Financial World* magazine named BankAmerica one of the ten worst-managed companies in America. The citation was hardly flattering to Clausen:

> If BankAmerica Corporation's board had dipped into a fresh pool of banking talent to replace former president Samuel Armacost, instead of bringing retired chairman A. W. "Tom" Clausen out of mothballs, we might have left the beleaguered banking company off the list on the grounds that its troubles are already well known. Because the autocratic Clausen was largely responsible for the banking company's problems in the first place, however, it is incomprehensible that the directors would have picked him to lead it out of the woods....
> We fail to see how someone so closely associated with the prob-

lem, which by year-end will have produced $2 billion in losses over the past three years, can be part of the solution....

Journalist Gary Hector, in his valuable and incisive book, *Breaking the Bank: The Decline of BankAmerica*, also had many critical words to say about Clausen, a good many of them quite appropriate. He ended his book in a decidedly downbeat manner, stating that "The bank that A. P. Giannini had built was dead. It was Tom Clausen's bank now."

Well, that certainly was true, it was Tom Clausen's bank and much to the surprise of banking and business community—including, I must confess, this writer—he proceeded to engineer one of the great turnarounds in the history of banking on second thought, make that in the history of American business.

What BankAmerica Did

In the 1986 annual report, within a few months after he had returned to the bank, Clausen outlined an ambitious plan for recovery:

> Our recovery program is based upon a simple premise: we will focus on the basic banking business which has been the cornerstone of this institution for more than 80 years.
>
> We will be the premier provider of retail and wholesale banking services in the Western United States, and we will be a preeminent wholesale bank offering a focused package of networth and capital market services in the United States and world markets....
>
> This focused strategy also lays the groundwork for the other steps necessary to restructure our operations in order to return to profitability:
>
> ■ We anticipate continued improvement in the performance of our credit portfolio.
>
> ■ We will continue to divest businesses and operations which are not essential to our strategic objectives, thereby enhancing BankAmerica's capital resources.
>
> ■ We plan to significantly reduce expenses, especially in any area that does not support the delivery of quality products and services to our customers and clients.
>
> ■ We intend to raise additional capital, including the issuance of equity securities, to support the future growth of our core businesses and strengthen our capital base.
>
> ■ We are using the technology being developed by our BankAmerica Systems Engineering group to improve quality of service to our customers and to make our own operations more efficient and effective.

The recovery plan covers some of the deficiencies of the Clausen operations during the 1970s. It also sounds somewhat familiar, doesn't it? It seems a little like the five-point program John Reed enunciated for Citicorp at the end of 1990.

During 1987, the loss widened and probably would have widened more had a more realistic provision been made for losses on the bank's Latin American portfolio. Assets and deposits also were down, but the primary and total capital increased. Early in the year, the board rejected the merger proposal from First Interstate, and the offer was withdrawn a month later.

Progress on most of the recovery plan fronts was reported, although a case could be made that some of the credit should have gone to Thomas A. Cooper, the president and chief operating officer; he and Clausen did not get along, and Cooper left during the year.

But one of the best moves Clausen made was to bring in Richard A. Rosenberg as vice chairman and head of the California banking group. Rosenberg had been president of Seafirst where he was credited with strengthening that subsidiary of BankAmerica.

Progress continued during 1988, with the bank returning to profitability and an increase in loans, deposits, and assets. At the time, Clausen stated that, while pleased with the progress made, "we are acutely aware of how much work is yet to be done and how much challenge the problems and opportunities before us contain."

With profits hitting $1.1 billion, the highest in the bank's history, 1989 proved to be a watershed year; interest income was up; and loans, deposits, and assets were up. Risk-based capital also increased and was already well above the minimum guidelines mandated for the end of 1992.

Clausen was justifiably proud of what he had engineered. In the annual report, he made this statement:

> We are aggressively back in our markets, have an excellent management team, and a strategy which I am confident is not only achievable, but is the proper one to carry BankAmerica successfully into the nineties.
>
> On the basis of this record, then, I believe it is safe to conclude that the task laid out by the Board of Directors when it asked me to return to retake the helm of BankAmerica in October of 1986 has been completed.
>
> The turnaround has been accomplished. The recovery is a fact. The corporation has competitive momentum and is on a winning track.
>
> My job is done. Therefore, I will take my leave of BankAmerica again. I will retire from the active management of the corporation effective at the close of the annual shareholders meeting on May 24, 1990.

He also stated that Richard Rosenberg, who had recently been made president, would succeed him as chairman and chief executive officer at that time.

Handing Off the Baton

Tom Clausen had come back for three and one-half years and had helped return BankAmerica to a position of strength. Considering the terrible condition BankAmerica was in when he did return, the turnaround was nothing sort of remarkable.

Since that time, Richard Rosenberg has been aggressively moving his bank forward. After a year as chairman, he said, "With solid capital resources and a dedicated, motivated, and proven staff, BankAmerica is now in position to take advantage of growth opportunities in geographic market areas which have the potential for increasing and delivering our revenue generation, and with it, our profitability."

Obviously, Dick Rosenberg is wasting no time in taking advantage of those growth opportunities, acting decisively and with a sense of purpose.

Now, Citicorp

Citicorp was never in as bad a shape as BankAmerica, and its problems surfaced later. However, BankAmerica's board saw what it had to do; that a new management team had to be brought in, albeit a partially recycled one. Then the new management acted decisively on a number of fronts, and it continues to act that same way even after getting back on track. Rosenberg obviously realized he must seize the opportunities that present themselves without delay and in a positive manner.

Citicorp's problem is that it waited far too long before taking action. It did follow the course of action laid out by Clausen and his people at BankAmerica. And in some of the areas it has moved rather aggressively.

However, so much more must be done. The corporation's capital base is still weak, and one wonders if it has the will to do what is necessary to build it up. Yes, John Reed says that Citi understands the need for strong capital, that it has changed its position on this. But the question lingers as to how much change has actually taken place.

One of the big differences between Citicorp and BankAmerica is the awful real estate loan portfolio Citi had—and still has. In some respects, there is only so much the bank can do to solve the problem. There is only so much real estate it can take over and hold on to before that by itself becomes stifling.

Costs are being cut, and this is good. The number of employees continues to be reduced, and this step is absolutely necessary.

But other questions remain. Is the management team being effectively and sufficiently strengthened? Are the core businesses being expanded as much as possible? Is enough being done to get rid of noncore assets? Does management understand that the financial marketplace is changing, the configurations are different, and the competition is moving forward with renewed vigor and determination?

Is Citicorp in reality becoming a leaner, meaner organization, the kind of organization it must become to successfully move through the rest of the twentieth century and into the twenty-first? The answer at this stage can only be a resounding "maybe."

14

Citicorp's World in the Twenty-First Century

It is always hazardous to make predictions, particularly when it involves an unpredictable corporation such as Citicorp and such a volatile industry as banking. At the same time, one must have the courage of his or her convictions and provide an astute analysis of the situation. Moreover, making predictions can be a lot of fun. And if the predictor is right (or mostly right), the fearless forecaster can point with pride at being so incisive and all-knowing. Of course, if the time frame is sufficiently long—and this one in regard to Citicorp is—almost no one (except enemies and other similarly suspect people) will call a person on his or her wrong guesses.

So, based on these premises, the following are my predictions about Citicorp and what it will be like in the twenty-first century, meaning after 1999. Please note, that this is the only time frame this seer is willing to make; some of the predictions could well take place later—or much sooner, maybe even before you read this book.

Will Citicorp still be around in the year 2000?
Yes.

Will it be the same then as it is now?
No.

Will it be bigger than it is now?
Probably, but not necessarily all that much.

What bank will be the largest bank in the United States?
Not Citicorp.

Come the year 2000, will Citi still be the largest bank in New York City?
It could be, particularly if it merges with a stronger bank.

Will money-center banks still be important?
Sure, but probably not as important as the superregionals.

Will Citicorp still be important on the international banking scene?
Probably, but maybe not *as* important.

Will Citicorp still be important domestically?
Probably, but maybe not *as* important.

Will Citicorp's stock be higher or lower than it is the day you read this?
Who knows? Certainly not Ross Perot.

Who will be in charge of Citicorp?
Not John Reed.

Index

About the Author

Richard B. Miller is a veteran financial and banking journalist who has reported on the banking industry for over 25 years. Formerly the editor of *The Bankers Magazine* and *Bankers Monthly*, he has kept a keen watch on Citicorp's activities. He is the author of a dozen books on financial topics, including *American Banking in Crisis, Super Banking, The Bankers Desk Book,* and *The Banking Jungle* (coauthored with Paul Nadler).